CHELSEA
AZZURRI

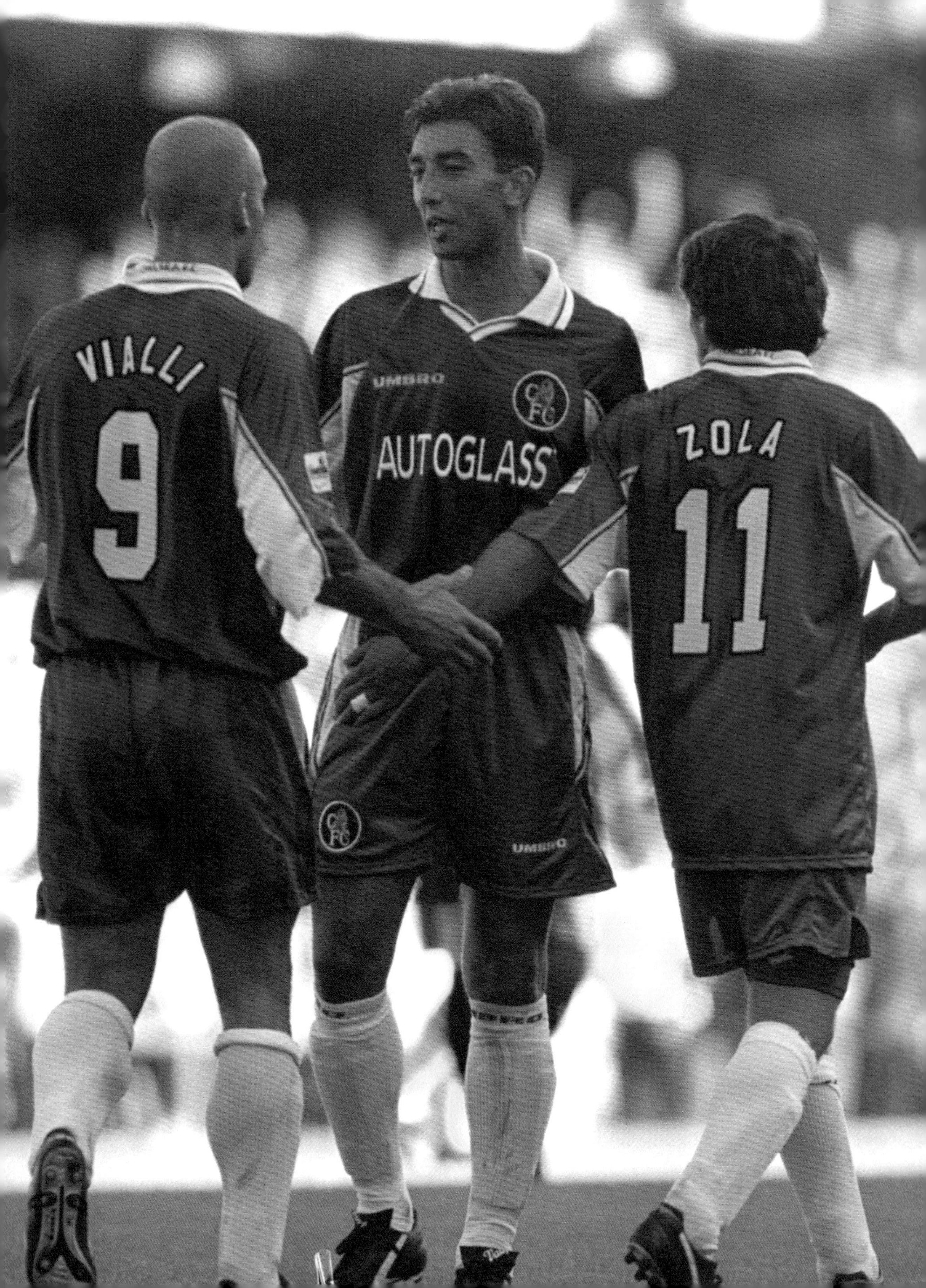
VIALLI
9
UMBRO
AUTOGLASS
ZOLA
11
UMBRO

CHELSEA
AZZURRI

RUUD GULLIT'S
BLUE REVOLUTION

Text by Brian Scovell

Photographs by Dave Shopland

Foreword by Peter Osgood

CollinsWillow
An Imprint of HarperCollins*Publishers*

First published in 1997 by CollinsWillow
an imprint of HarperCollins*Publishers*
London

© Brian Scovell and Dave Shopland 1997

1 3 5 7 9 8 6 4 2

A CIP catalogue record for this book
is available from the British Library

ISBN 0 00 218799 X (paperback)
ISBN 0 00 218807 4 (hardback)

Additional photographs by Andy Hooper and Coloursport

Printed in Great Britain by The Bath Press

This is not an official publication of Chelsea Football Club

CONTENTS

WHY I AM SO PROUD OF CHELSEA

by Peter Osgood

There was no-one more proud of Chelsea's achievement in winning the FA Cup in 1997 than me. I played in three finals in three years with them as a player, but that day beat everything. It was like a graduation day, the day that my club came out with all the honours and could now compete with the very best clubs in world football.

There is no player anywhere who would want to turn down the chance to come to Chelsea. At long last we were in a position to challenge Manchester United.

I turned down all interviews before the Final because I just wanted to go as a fan with my wife Lynne who was visiting Wembley for the first time. It was a wonderful, wonderful day and when we went to the reception at the Waldorf in the evening and met Pele, it rounded things off nicely.

We won the FA Cup in 1970 with a side which would, I believe, give today's side a very close game, but the club failed to capitalise on it and things started going downhill. They got their priorities wrong. This time I cannot see that happening. In four years Stamford Bridge has been transformed from a shambles into one of the world's greatest grounds. The money is there to finance the rebuilding.

Ruud Gullit can bring in the big name players he wants to improve the side and the squad is big enough and good enough to meet the demands of playing in four competitions. The football they are playing is exciting and I get the same buzz as the supporters. It is a great time to be a Chelsea fan. I firmly believe the club will go on to better things.

Peter Osgood in action for Chelsea (LEFT) and before the 1997 Cup Final against Middlesbrough (INSET) with another former Stamford Bridge favourite, Kerry Dixon.

VISITING TEA

THE RUUD REVOLUTION

Ruud Gullit had never managed or coached at any level when he was appointed Chelsea manager at the start of the 1996-97 season. But such was his influence that by the end of it he had transformed the club from chronic under-achievers with a loyal, passionate following into winners worthy of competing at the highest peaks of European football.

Twenty-six barren years ended with victory in the FA Cup Final at Wembley. By moulding his own ideas, picked up at a string of championship-winning clubs in Holland and Italy, with the traditional values of English football, Gullit created a new style, one that appealed to followers not just in West London but throughout the country. His purchase of a stable of quality players like Gianfranco Zola, the 1996-97 Footballer of the Year, Gianluca Vialli, Roberto Di Matteo and Frank Leboeuf, soon to be followed by others, excited the nation. It was a revolution that others wanted to copy.

Not that Gullit was a firebrand. He was calm and relaxed, so much so that those watching him lounging in the dugout wondered whether he really cared about what went on out there. 'I can only remember losing my temper once,' Gullit recalled. 'It was at the game at Spurs when we didn't

'The only silverware on view was the chairman's beard!'

play well. I don't believe in being loud. It is not my style.'

The changes on the field were accompanied by dramatic improvements off it. The rebuilding of Stamford Bridge, and the development of a complex that included a hotel, flats and a huge underground car park, put Chelsea at the forefront of the nation's football clubs. No longer was Chelsea FC the butt of comedians.

When Ken Bates took over as chairman in 1982 from Viscount Chelsea - he paid a token £1 to take over the club - they were 12th in the old Second Division and Clive Walker was the leading scorer in the League with sixteen goals. It somehow seems ironic that fifteen years on, Walker is still playing in the Vauxhall Conference, and still scoring goals. In those days Chelsea really were a joke. The erratic Yugoslav Petar Borota was in goal and the main defender was the giant Mickey Droy, a popular figure but no Frank Leboeuf.

The following season, then manager John Neal and his assistant Ian McNeil managed to avoid relegation before taking the club back to the First Division in 1983-84, chiefly through the 28 goals of Kerry Dixon. McNeil recalls that Bates was constantly on the phone to Neal, urging him to buy this player and that player. The snag was that there was little or no money.

Except for one League title in 1954-55, achieved with the lowest winning points total, 52, since the First World War, there had been little to show for all the flamboyance of Chelsea's football. The sole title success was achieved

by an average side in an average year. It was followed by the club's only success in the FA Cup in 1970, and a year later by victory in the Final of the European Cup-Winners' Cup. Throw in a solitary success in the Football League Cup in 1964-65 and two successes in the Full Members Cup in 1986 and 1990 (by which time it was called the Zenith Data Systems Trophy) and that was the extent of the club's trophy room. No wonder one cynic observed: 'The only silverware on view was the chairman's beard!'

For most of his time in charge the abrasive, single-minded Bates had fought a rearguard action to preserve Stamford Bridge, a prime building site, from the developers. Several times he came close to defeat. Supporters were asked to contribute to the 'Save the Bridge' Fund. Against the odds, Bates managed to save the club and when the last decade of the twentieth century started, the pendulum began swinging the other way.

A key appointment was the recruiting of Glenn Hoddle as manager in the summer of 1993. Hoddle was 35 at the time and still player-manager of Swindon. Bates liked the way he had Swindon playing: they were a passing side which scored plenty of goals. Though basically unqualified, Hoddle had firm ideas about how he wanted the game played, many of them learned during his spell at Monaco when he worked under Arsene Wenger. David Webb, who scored the winning goal in the FA Cup Final replay against Leeds in 1970, had

been in temporary charge at the Bridge and thought he had done enough to keep the job. But Bates wanted the club to return to its traditions of playing exciting football and Hoddle was still the best passer in England.

Hoddle quickly made changes, putting the emphasis on improved fitness standards, proper diets and a more responsible attitude from the players. The 1970 side had earned a reputation for rakish behaviour and heavy drinking. He wanted to rid the club of any lingering leftover of that.

The then-chairman Brian Mears used to joke that various publicans

would ring him up, saying that some of the players were still drinking and they wanted to close up for the night. 'I am afraid that is not my responsibility,' he would reply. 'It's the manager's.'

Hoddle improved the style of the team but soon realised he did not have good enough players to take it to the levels he and Ken Bates had outlined when they first met. Some of the players he bought, as Bates would claim later, were poor value for money. By this time the system of transferring players in Europe was changing as clubs accepted that once the Belgian player Jean Marc

Bosman had won his court case, as he assuredly would, players would be able to move at the end of their contracts without their club receiving a transfer fee. It opened up a new vista in English football: the top clubs would be able to compete with the richest clubs in Spain, Germany and Italy to recruit world-class stars. With the pay-outs now available from BSkyB's new deal with the Premier League, English clubs were actually in a stronger financial position than their rivals on the Continent. Many leading clubs in Italy and Spain were heavily in debt. Wages were far too high and TV income was meagre in comparison.

Chelsea were among the first clubs to recognise the advantages of signing older, experienced players who could bring extra qualities to the still very predictable English game, which remained dominated by the long ball, offside tactics and aerial combat around the penalty areas.

Hoddle had first encountered Ruud Gullit while playing for Tottenham against Feyenoord in 1983. Gullit was 19 and was used in the role of sweeper.

Peter Shreeves, the Tottenham coach, remembered: 'We tried to buy him around that time but his agent thought it was too early in

Bates wanted the club to return to its traditions of playing exciting football and Hoddle was still the best passer in England.

his career to play abroad and he was probably right.' The Arsenal manager Terry Neill had been offered him a couple of years earlier. 'He looked like another Duncan Edwards except that he was much quicker, much more skilful,' said Neill.

Ruud Gullit was born on September 1, 1962, the son of George Gullit, a former Surinam international footballer, coach and teacher, and Ria Dil, a Dutchwoman. His parents split up and when his father returned to his homeland, Ruud took the name of Rudi Dil. It was a sign of his tremendous self-belief and independent spirit when, at the age of thirteen, he decided that Rudi Dil did not sound right for the name of a footballer. So he decided to alter his Christian name to Ruud and adopt his father's name. From that moment on, he was Ruud Gullit. At Chelsea most of those close to him call him Rudi, including some of the players.

In his early teens he trained at non-League club DWS near his home in Amsterdam in preference to Ajax, Anderlecht and a host of other clubs who wanted to sign him. An Englishman, Barry Hughes, was the first to recognise his talents, and George Gullit accepted Hughes's offer for Ruud to sign for FC Haarlem because Hughes promised a bonus of £500 if Ruud passed his examinations at school. A teacher himself, George Gullit was more impressed with that gesture than he was by bigger offers from richer, more established clubs. His son was an intelligent boy, already capable of conversing in several languages.

Ruud was the youngest-ever Dutch footballer to make his League debut when he played for Haarlem as a centre-half on August 19, 1979. By the end of the year he had been shifted forward into attack to help his club back into the First Division. He then moved to Feyenoord and was briefly in the same side as the legendary Johan Cruyff. By 1985 when he transferred to PSV Eindhoven, Gullit was earning £8,000 a week, making him the highest-paid player in the country. Off the field, his personality and appeal to the public earned him almost as much.

His independent streak was revealed again as he fell out with the PSV management before he was sold to AC Milan in 1987 for a then world record fee of £5.5 million. Milan coach Arrigo Sacchi used him as a midfield player and he excelled to such an extent that Milan won the title in 1988 and the following year they won the European Cup. During the 1987-88 season Gullit was voted World and European Footballer of the Year. Honours and medals continued to come his way, but so did the disputes both with Milan and Holland, whom he had inspired to success in the 1988 European Championships. He also had to undergo a series of operations on his right knee.

Gullit was experiencing a quieter life with Sampdoria when Chelsea heard in the spring of 1995 that he might be available on a free transfer. Hoddle flew to Milan, accompanied by the club's managing director Colin Hutchinson, to meet him and discovered that it was a meeting of like minds. Gullit promised to speak again later. On the same trip, Hoddle and Hutchinson went to Rome to agree a £4.25m deal with Lazio's president Sergio Cragnotti to take Paul Gascoigne back to the Premiership.

'We talked things over with Gazza over dinner and there were a few jokes, especially when Gazza swallowed one of his crowns that had just been fitted,' said Hutchinson. 'But we came away thinking he didn't really want to play for Chelsea.' That feeling was soon confirmed when Gascoigne signed for Glasgow Rangers. Ten days later Hutchinson returned to Milan to clinch a two-year deal with Gullit. On Bank Holiday Monday, May 29, Hutchinson was watching the Bolton v Reading First Division play-off final when Gullit rang to confirm that he had approved the deal. 'One of the reasons he signed,' Hutchinson said, 'was that Chelsea played in white socks, and he always won things playing for teams in white socks!' Galatasaray, managed by Graeme Souness, Bayern Munich, Tottenham, QPR and at least one Japanese club all wanted to sign him. But Gullit chose London because of what it had to offer as a cosmopolitan city and because it was a short flying distance from his children in Amsterdam. 'I followed my instinct,' he said.

When he arrived at Stamford Bridge on June 22, 1995 for a press conference, there was a massive turn-out of media representatives. He delighted them all with his readiness to speak on any subject, even mimicking the Cockney accents of Dennis Wise and Peter Shreeves. Gullitmania had taken over by the time he made his first appearance in a

> **'One of the reasons he signed was that Chelsea played in white socks, and he always won things playing for teams in white socks!'**

Chelsea shirt, in a pre-season friendly at Gillingham. The gates were locked and hundreds of fans outside went home disappointed. He made his League debut against Everton in a 0-0 draw in front of another capacity crowd. 'My goal is only to play good football,' he said. 'We have a good team at Chelsea, but it is a young team. If you like, we are like virgins, getting to know each other. I never think of what I want to win, just to have a good time with my football. If you are playing good, enjoyable football then the trophies will take care of themselves.'

It was a new kind of philosophy for English players brought up on the demands of winning at almost any cost. Gullit's first season was hailed as an unqualified success with attendances at Stamford Bridge rising 20 per cent despite a lowering in the capacity caused by the rebuilding work. He started as sweeper, the position he had agreed upon with Hoddle, and later played in midfield, wide on the right and up front. Yet for all his class, all the sparkle he brought to the side, Chelsea still finished in a moderate 11th place

and his tally of three goals in 31 League matches was a low one. In the FA Cup his record was better, with three goals including one in the semi-final where Chelsea lost to Manchester United.

By the end of the season the FA were running short of candidates to succeed Terry Venables as England coach. Jimmy Armfield, their advisor, had been turned down by a clutch of managers

including former England captains Gerry Francis, Bryan Robson and Kevin Keegan. None of the successful, established managers, such as Alex Ferguson, wanted the post either. One of the few who was keen was Hoddle and to the dismay of Bates, his man agreed to take it. Hoddle was inexperienced, unqualified in terms of FA coaching certificates and none too well-versed in public relations. He had none of the confidence of Venables in front of a mike. But his sincerity and his love of good football came through whenever he spoke.

Bates did not bother to draw up a short list. He had already made up his mind to offer Gullit the chance to take over as player-manager and the indications from the club's supporters were that they were totally in favour. After two hours of talks with Hutchinson on May 10, Gullit agreed to the new arrangement on exactly the same pay (around £16,000 a week) he was earning as a player. The club extended his two-year contract by a further year. Gullit's mission was to coach the team and impart the ideas he had picked up in Holland, Italy and every other country he had played in, and also to tell Bates and Hutchinson which players he wanted to bring to the club. It would then be up to the directors to do the negotiations.

FROM LEFT: Frank Leboeuf, Erland Johnsen, Jody Morris, Roberto Di Matteo, Dennis Wise and Dan Petrescu celebrate the first League goal under Gullit with an early contender for goal celebration of the season.

GULLIT ON TAKING THE JOB

'I am not stressed about it. I have won everything. I am a happy man. But they insisted I have the job and I thought I would enjoy coaching and helping the players. I have no pressure whatsoever. What can I lose?'

Gullit insisted the team play in a similar way to the style employed by Hoddle. 'I am not trying to make it a Continental style,' he said. 'I want to use the best of both styles.'

The players soon discovered that his being the boss did not change Gullit's manner. He was just as approachable, just as much one of them, except now they had to carry out his orders. Dennis Wise said: 'He's a great fellow, a lovely man. What happened when he first came was that the lads were in awe of him. We thought he would do everything, all we had to do was give him the ball. But it wasn't long before he was one of the lads. He doesn't walk around thinking he is above us.'

He was always willing to join in the jokes and the repartee. But underneath the laughter and the fun was a serious message: that if you didn't work, you wouldn't stay in the side. Training was more intensified. The strikers in

particular were grateful to him for the tips he passed on. John Spencer's game improved as a result, but there were other players beyond help. He was critical when he had to be, in a supportive fashion, saying: 'Your best friend is a friend who can be negative, who can say: "I don't want you to do that."'

He was not slow to pick up the footballing vernacular either. He once called Hoddle 'the gaffer', and made the journalists laugh after one match when he said: 'We struggled a bit, early doors.' A smile was never far away as the Chelsea manager sat back to dissect matches and performances. On countless occasions he was asked: 'How do you stand up to the pressure?'

'What pressure?' he asked. 'I don't feel any. I have a happy life and what happens on the pitch will not change that. Everyone gets rid of their nerves in a different way. Other managers may get up and shout, but I like to be relaxed.

FAR LEFT: Gullit with his assistant manager, Graham Rix. The former Arsenal midfielder has often played a key role in the team's tactical approach.

ABOVE: Feet up, Ruud relaxes as those around him take the strain. It was his standard position during matches. Rix (second from left) usually stood.

Great players are rarely injured, it is said, chiefly because they have the ability to see danger before it threatens and the skill to ride tackles. When Ruud Gullit's season ended at Derby early in March 1997, it was an accident – and even the great players cannot prevent accidents happening.

The injury to his ankle occurred when he tripped and caught an opponent's foot as he fell. A scan later revealed he had a hairline fracture of the ankle. A younger player might have recovered, certainly for the FA Cup Final. But Gullit was unconcerned. 'I am in no hurry,' he said. At his age, 34, he knew he risked permanent damage if he came back too soon.

'I don't watch the game as a supporter,' Gullit explained. 'I am not following the ball. I am watching the moods and behaviour of my players. Sure I get tense sometimes, but I am used to living with pressure. It is more of a problem with other people than me. Maybe if we hadn't done so well, people would look at me with my legs stretched out and say, "He doesn't care enough." But I work the way I do.

'I do not think about winning trophies. I have never in my life stopped to sit down at home and think about all the trophies I have won. I never feel satisfied. No-one in football should feel satisfied. They should all be seeking to better themselves.

'My philosophy is to think of the next match and put out a team that plays good football and which wins. Trophies can come if you do that. What really gives me a good feeling is that Chelsea are being talked about all over Europe for the way they play. That makes me proud, seeing my players develop.'

Wise summed up Gullit's management style when he said: 'He is so laid-back. He is not the type to go kicking cups around the dressing-room. He doesn't lose his rag but if he is annoyed, you soon get the message because he tells you straight to your face. He wants us to enjoy playing every game, but he also wants us to be ruthless to achieve everything.'

LEFT: The master in control, as he toys with Teddy Sheringham and David Howells (right) of Spurs. Gullit scored the opening goal in Chelsea's 3-1 victory which the team dedicated to Matthew Harding.

RIGHT: Gullit is helped off the pitch at the Baseball Ground. An apparently innocuous fall left him with a broken ankle and ended his playing season. Chelsea lost the game 3-2.

There were things that upset Gullit and the chief one was his side's seeming inability to defeat lower sides on a consistent basis. 'That was our weakness,' he said. 'Good teams will always beat inferior teams, but with us that was not so. If we had picked up the points we should have done against these teams, we would have qualified for Europe before we won the FA Cup.'

There was also the time when he criticised his players' attitude in the 3-0 home defeat by Arsenal. Asked about it later, Gullit explained: 'I did it to get a response. I sought confrontation because I knew good players would react, and they did. It is something that has always been a part of the mentality of Dutch teams. You criticise them and they come back and play better. It is part of football.'

By aiming the goals of his players as high as possible, he helped make them better players. 'Before I became coach, I thought there was maybe more talent in the team than they showed,' he said. 'They are doing things now that they did not know they had in them. I just wanted to keep them doing things in my own way, in the way I have been doing them throughout my career. I am happy with the progress we have made. But it can be better. There is more to come.'

Former England coach Don Howe has always said that different clubs have distinctive styles peculiar to them. Arsenal, for example, base their success on a sound defensive system, Manchester United put the emphasis on attacking flair and pace out of defence, Wimbledon on the early ball forward. Chelsea's style, according to Howe, was always on the erratic side, a mixture of the best and the worst.

'Whether we like it or not,' he said, 'managers and players come and go but the clubs retain their tradition. Look at Tottenham.

They have always been push and run. Gerry Francis has tried to some extent to change that, but I am not sure how successful he has been.

'I am happy with the progress we have made. But it can be better. There is more to come.'

'Chelsea have always been entertaining and inconsistent. Look at Dave Sexton's team with Osgood, Hudson and Webby. Everybody knew they were a beautiful football team, but they were never consistent enough to win the title. It is no good being able to put four magnificent

games together and then play four more upside down.

'That character seems to stick. I would think that even now Ruud is saying, "We are not consistent enough. On our day we can beat the best but we cannot maintain that consistency." I bet if you went back to Ted Drake he would have been saying exactly the same before he won the title in 1955.

'I think Chelsea can change it. Not forever, but for a year or two like in 1955. Then sooner or later they will go back. It is like a flower. It has a base colour. It will go yellow and go red, but it will go back to be purple in a few years' time. At some stage someone will say, "That is our club, that is the way we play."'

The real measure of Gullit's achievement as a coach was to change substantially the playing mode and turn Chelsea into a pedigree passing side with an infinite variety of attacking options. As yet he has been unable to eradicate totally the age-long inconsistency because it is too inbred. But he is working on it . . . and he usually gets his way.

LEFT: Gullit salutes the fans at the Cup Final with a clenched fist and the promise of more trophies to come.

FAR LEFT: A new season, a new challenge. Ruud and his players look relaxed at a 1997 pre-season game v Reading.

THE RUUD REVOLUTION

THE FOREIGN LEGION

Gianfranco Zola arrived at Chelsea in mid-November 1997 when English football was searching for a hero. The previous two winners of the Footballer of the Year Award were both foreigners, Eric Cantona and Jurgen Klinsmann. Cantona may have earned the public's respect but arguably not their love or esteem. And Klinsmann had returned to Germany before he could build on his success.

The phlegmatic Alan Shearer was the choice of the players as the 1996-97 PFA Player of the Year and though he deserved recognition for his consistent goalscoring exploits, he failed to captivate the fans as a personality. When he spoke in public, it was rarely with a smile or any sign of exuberance. It was as if he wasn't really enjoying it unless he was scoring goals.

Franco Zola soon changed everyone's perception of what a sporting idol should be like. He gave the appearance of enjoying what he did and he smiled easily and often, delighting those who approached him for an autograph, or a favour. The English press were overwhelmed by him. Here was a top player who actually wanted to talk at length to them, without demanding any payment or suggesting a call to an agent. When the interview was over, he would extend his hand and say:

'Thank you.' His English, fractured and rudimentary at first, rapidly improved. He soon became very popular, not just with Chelsea fans but with supporters throughout the country.

Here was a simple man, from humble origins in Sardinia, giving a lesson in deportment and manners to every professional sportsman in the land. His talent on the pitch justified the laudatory notices he was receiving. 'He can unlock the door,' said Ruud Gullit. 'These players are invaluable and there are not many of them.'

Zola's control, change of pace,

and ability to beat defenders were of the highest standard. His runs were brilliantly timed and inventive. And he had the rare gift of almost perfect balance which only players like George Best, Pele and Diego Maradona possessed. Balance is what enables great players to evade tackles and keep possession of the ball. On top of all this, Zola could score marvellously crafted goals, like the ones he scored against Wimbledon in the FA Cup semi-final when he wrong-footed Dean Blackwell, and the one he scored for Italy against England at Wembley.

Instead of retarding his popularity, that winning goal at Wembley seemed only to enhance the affection the English public had for him. Here at last was a genuine hero: a thoroughly nice, uncomplicated man who personified all the right values. He was happily married with two young children and in his spare time practised playing the piano. He had fun on the Internet and he liked taking his family to London's tourist spots.

Middlesbrough's Juninho was his chief rival for the award and he, too, was popular with managers, coaches and supporters alike. His club might have been relegated but he never stopped entertaining the fans and trying to rouse those around him. It should have been a close race, but it wasn't. When the votes were counted in the Footballer of the Year poll conducted by the nation's 350 football journalists and broadcasters, Zola won twice as many votes as Juninho, with his team-mate Mark Hughes one vote behind the Brazilian.

FAR LEFT: A rare example of the Football Writers' Player of the Year heading the ball. Newcastle's Alan Shearer watches in amazement.

LEFT: On Cup Final day, the temperature was in the high seventies at Wembley and a man needs to cool down!

Zola's victory in the writers' poll was proof that in the modern era of image, it is important to smile and appear nice. Politicians like Bill Clinton and Tony Blair have teams working on their image, advising them what to say and what not to say. Zola succeeded firstly because he is a very fine player and secondly because he is a natural. He doesn't have to appear nice, he is nice. And it was a pleasant change to

see someone at the very top of his sport showing genuine humility. His size helped. There is always extra goodwill for someone small of stature, a little man taking on big men and winning.

The way the world is changing, there must now be doubts whether the most advanced nations of the world will ever again produce a naturally gifted world-class footballer. Youngsters growing up in these countries are more

proficient at video games and working computers than they are at controlling a football.

The great players, the ones who work on their skills for countless hours, will continue to come from

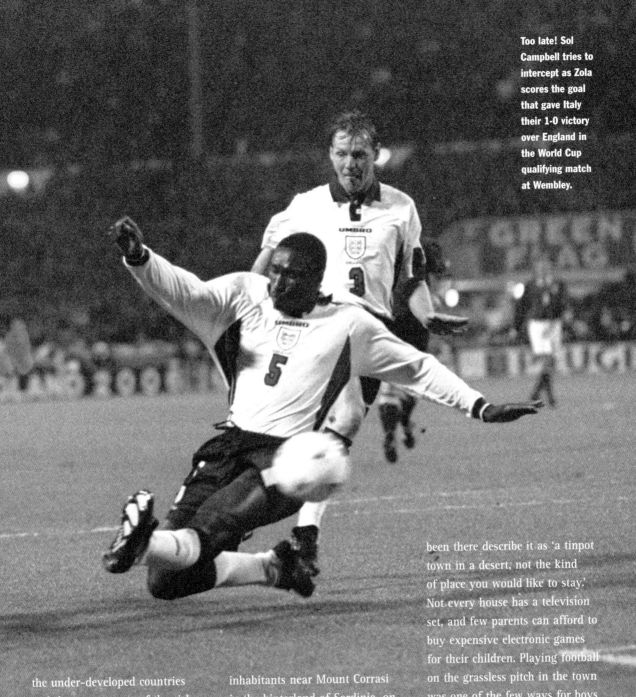

the under-developed countries and the poorer parts of the richer nations until they, too, are overtaken by technology.

Gianfranco Zola was born in Oliena, a small town of 8,000 inhabitants near Mount Corrasi in the hinterland of Sardinia, on July 5, 1966, just a few days before the World Cup tournament started in England. Visitors, and there are not many, who have been there describe it as 'a tinpot town in a desert, not the kind of place you would like to stay.' Not every house has a television set, and few parents can afford to buy expensive electronic games for their children. Playing football on the grassless pitch in the town was one of the few ways for boys to pass their time in 1966. There are more distractions today but football remains a readily available option.

'I PREFER MY WIFE!'

One of Zola's least successful matches was the 2-2 draw at home against Sheffield Wednesday. Before the game, Wednesday manager David Pleat toyed with the idea of asking his skipper Peter Atherton to man-mark Zola. 'I decided against it, and it proved to be the wrong decision,' he said.

After Zola (8 minutes) and Hughes (22) had put Chelsea ahead, Pleat signalled to Atherton to follow Zola everywhere and it became a different game. Mark Pembridge (23) beat Frode Grodas with a magnificent strike, and when the Norwegian fumbled a thirty-yard volley from Dejan Stefanovic over the line in the 90th minute, Wednesday managed to draw 2-2. Asked what he thought of Atherton's close attentions, Zola brought a roar of laughter from the assembled journalists when he said: 'I prefer my wife!'

He added: 'Being marked was no problem. I was used to it all the time in Italy. But having played a match two days earlier, I was tired. Now I am going home to bed!

'In Italy we say it is a game for men. I am 30, not a child. In Italy some players were rude to me but I have not had that here. If there is a problem, I call for Mark Hughes. I say, "Marco, come here!" Then there is no problem!'

Ingazio Zola, Franco's father, is a 66-year-old, wizened little man of a little over five feet who owns the Bar Sport in Oliena. A former footballer himself, he ran the Bar Sport football team for many years – most of its players were relatives. He was also president of Corrasi, the local football club.

'Franco was kicking any object in his path from the age of nine months, so we gave him a football as a present for his first birthday,' he said. 'He has been devoted to the game ever since. He was always kicking the ball against the walls outside our bar for hours on end. He never wanted to do anything else, only football mattered to him. I took him up to Corrasi when he was four because it was obvious he was going to be something special. A top Italian scout liked the way he kicked the ball at the age of eight and forecast that he would become a professional player. He was always much smaller than his team-mates but it never bothered him. He had a lot of confidence in his ability.'

Zola's background was similar to Diego Maradona's, and when they played together at Napoli he learned a lot from Maradona, who was six years older. Maradona was born in a working-class suburb of Buenos Aires, Avellaneda, in a hospital named after Eva Peron. His father, also named Diego, and mother Dona lived in a shanty.

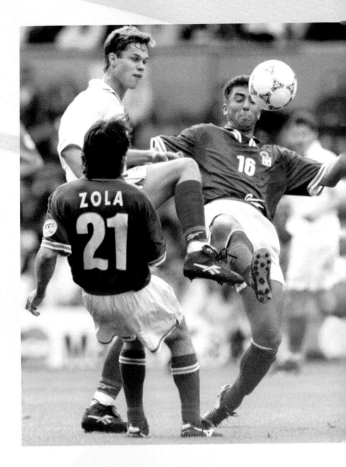

RIGHT: Future Chelsea team-mates Zola and Di Matteo in action for the other *Azzurri*, the Italian national side, during what was to prove a disappointing Euro 96 for them.

OPPOSITE: The fans' favourite acknowledges the crowd and shows the now famous number 25 shirt to the camera at the FA Cup Final.

Maradona's father was a poorly-paid porter who couldn't afford to give his son a football. Diego junior's first football was provided for him at the age of three by his uncle Cirilo. The Zola family was not as poor or deprived as Maradona's, but there was not much money to waste.

By the time he was fourteen, Zola was a regular in the Corrasi senior side. His father told the *Daily Express*: 'Bruno Conti of Roma was his boyhood hero but he learned most from Maradona during the time they played together at Napoli, especially how to perfect those free-kicks. I was there when he made his debut for Napoli against Inter in 1989. The crowd took to

'When Maradona left he insisted that Gianfranco should have his number ten jersey.'

him straightaway. They regarded him as Maradona's natural successor and so did he. When Maradona left in February 1991, he insisted that Gianfranco should have his number ten jersey.'

It was not an easy ride to the top for Zola junior. Cagliari, the Sardinian *Serie A* side, showed no interest in signing him and Nuorese, a club playing in the lower echelon of the Third Division, was his first professional club. They were relegated in his first season despite Zola's ten goals in 27 appearances. The following year he was back in the Third Division with another club, Torres, and his eight goals in 30 matches helped them gain promotion to the next league up, where he spent the next two seasons.

When he married his girlfriend Franca from the neighbouring town of Loculi, the couple spent their wedding night in a £20 room at the Kappa Hotel, half a mile from his father's bar. Vicenzo Palemodde, the hotel proprietor, says: 'Gianfranco has brought fame to this district and we are very grateful to him. His sister Silvia was a good player as well. She was a prolific goalscorer as a teenager.'

Even today there are occasional kidnappings in central Sardinia, and when one of his friends was abducted, Zola appealed for his release on TV and the bandits set the man free after a ransom was paid. Said Zola's father: 'We are a quiet, friendly people in this district and we like to spend time in and out of each other's houses. It is true there are some bandits around, but we have nothing to do with these people. They are outcasts.

'Gianfranco was never going to turn out that way. He never liked drinking, despite the fact that he lived in a bar and worked there when he was younger. He was often in bed by 9pm. He was always determined to make the top grade as a footballer.'

In 1989 Nello Barbanera, the sports director of Torres, persuaded Napoli's general manager Luciano Moggi to take a look at Zola, and Moggi, impressed by what he saw,

Zola's class was evident, but no-one watching him then would have thought he would eventually become a star in the English Premiership. He looked too small.

offered £200,000 for him. The offer was speedily accepted.

Napoli won the championship in Zola's first season, with the arrogant, self-destructive Maradona providing the motivational force, goals and controversy. Zola was 23. He appeared in 18 *Serie A* matches, scoring just twice. 'When I first met Maradona, it was like a flash of lightning,' he said. 'A player like Maradona will never be born again. I learned so much from watching him.'

In the summer of 1990 Zola was chosen for a Sardinian XI to take on an England XI when Bobby Robson was preparing his England squad for the World Cup Finals in Italy. The match took place in the crammed municipal stadium of Pula in Cagliari, and a weakened England side won 6-0 before an electric storm broke out over the city. On a hard, bumpy pitch, Zola's class was evident, but no-one watching him then would have thought he would eventually become a star in the English Premiership. He looked too small. Not many players of five feet five inches and ten and a half stone make the grade in England.

The game was dominated by the physical strength of players like Steve Bull, Steve McMahon and Des Walker. Only Walker, who was later to play in Italy himself, unsuccessfully, appeared regularly in England's World Cup matches in the tournament.

Zola's total of goals for Napoli was 32 in 105 appearances, a high ratio in a league in which defenders are the bosses. His first cap was against Norway and it was also the first game in charge for Arrigo Sacchi, the first Italian coach never to have played at any level of the game. Sacchi was a fitness and tactics man, not someone who appreciated the fantasy players; he and Zola never had much respect for each other.

THE UPS AND DOWNS OF GIANFRANCO ZOLA

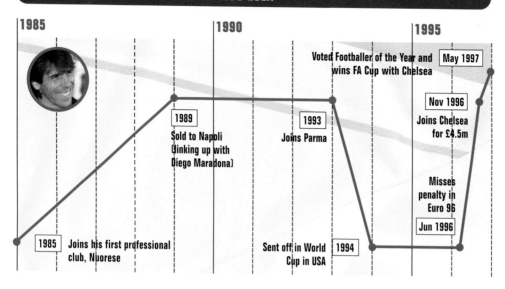

1985 **1990** **1995**

Voted Footballer of the Year and wins FA Cup with Chelsea — **May 1997**

Nov 1996
Joins Chelsea for £4.5m

1989
Sold to Napoli (linking up with Diego Maradona)

1993
Joins Parma

Misses penalty in Euro 96
Jun 1996

1985 Joins his first professional club, Nuorese

Sent off in World Cup in USA **1994**

Zola's international place was under threat after he was played out of position, wide on the right, for his new club Parma. When he first arrived there, the coach Nevio Scala was a Zola supporter but after Carlo Ancelotti took over, Zola's licence to have a free rein in attack was withdrawn. Ancelotti bought Enrico Chiesa and the Argentinian Herman Crespo, both forwards.

Zola realised he had to go. When Glenn Hoddle had inquired about him the previous season, Parma quoted a fee of £10 million. Now it was £4.5 million payable over five years at £1 million a year. Even with Zola's wages of almost £500,000 a year, it was still good business for Chelsea. Graham Rix, Gullit's assistant, recalls what happened when Zola

took part in his first training session. 'We had a keep-ball session and the standard is quite high,' he said. 'Franco joined in and was head-and-shoulders above everyone else. No-one could get the ball off him or even get near him. I am not sure I can teach him anything new. I try to keep him confident and the last thing I say to him when he goes on the pitch is: "Play with a smile on your face." He does, all the time. He hasn't come here just for the money. He wants to show people what he can do. His first touch is amazing. He has the ability to go forward while changing direction that the others can only dream about. If a defender dives in, boomph, he's away. Frightens them to death. I wish I had played with him.'

RIGHT: Zola holds off West Ham's Julian Dicks on his way to scoring a memorable goal for Chelsea at Stamford Bridge in December 1996. The little man's balance and control cannot be faulted. He's class!

It was one of Gianfranco Zola's proudest nights when he was presented with his Footballer of the Year trophy by Sir Stanley Matthews at the annual dinner of the Football Writers' Association on May 15, 1997. His natural charm, humility and humour won over an audience of 700 and he made one of the most memorable speeches by a recipient of the award.

'I don't know why you voted for me,' he said. 'I think you must be drunk.' The audience roared with laughter: the FWA dinner is known throughout the football industry as one of the biggest drinking nights of the calendar.

Sir Stanley was the first ever winner of the FWA award in 1947. 'I like watching him, he's such an entertaining little fellow,' was his verdict on Zola.

When the brief presentation ceremony ended at 10.10pm, chairman Joe Melling announced: 'Gentlemen, Gianfranco will now be leaving because he has an important engagement at Wembley. Ruud Gullit will be taking him home to put him to bed.'

Gullit turned to accompany the plain-clothes police officer assigned to protect Zola and suddenly realised that the little man was no longer next to him. Zola had gone down the line of sixteen past winners on the top table, shaking them by the hand. 'It was a lovely gesture,' said FWA chief executive Pat Signy. 'No winner has ever thought of doing that before. He's such a lovely man.'

Earlier, one of the officials, realising that the statuette, which weighs more than ten pounds, was weighing Zola down, said to him: 'Franco, let me hold that for you.' Zola smiled and replied: 'No, that's mine!'

LEFT: A smile that captivated the sporting nation: Zola's natural charm and sincerity instantly won over the audience when he received his Footballer of the Year award.

Zola soon found an Italian restaurant near his home which serves Sardinian-style Italian food. 'One thing that favours Italian players coming here is the number of Italian restaurants,' said former Chelsea captain Ray Wilkins, who had a long spell in Italy. 'They can go out in the evening and feel relaxed while talking their own language. I know how important that can be.'

Each week Zola received up to 1,000 letters from fans. 'He answered every one himself,' said Gwyn Williams, Chelsea's chief administrative officer. After an unexceptional start in the Premiership, Zola's confidence soared when he scored his opening goal in his third match, the 2-2 home draw against Everton. Typically it was a thirty-yard free-kick. Another goal against West Ham and two more in the 2-0 win at Aston Villa followed. He was on his way into the nation's hearts.

His international career has been blighted by controversy and it is only since Cesare Maldini took over as coach that his form has blossomed again. In the 1994 World Cup in the USA he was sent off in a bruising match against Nigeria soon after coming on as a substitute. 'I did not foul the player,' he maintained. 'I missed the rest of the tournament because of it, and I was still more upset when the secretary-general of FIFA, Sepp Blatter, said I deserved to go off.' It was a miserable 28th birthday for him.

Zola was back in the national team for Euro 96 in England, and again there was frustration and disappointment for him. After an exciting performance against Russia, he was demoted along with four other players for the second match against the Czech Republic and came on as a late substitute. Sacchi's decision to field a weakened side cost him dearly because it meant Italy, one of the favourites, had to beat eventual winners Germany in the third round of group matches to survive. They failed to do so.

The game was played at Old Trafford and in the eighth minute the Italians were awarded a penalty. Zola took it but his tame shot was turned round a post. The game ended 0-0 and Italy were out. So, it transpired, was Sacchi.

Zola's reincarnation as a top-flight international player occurred at Wembley on February 12, 1997 when he scored the only goal of the game against England and was voted Man of the Match. As Stuart Pearce hesitated, briefly raising an arm to appeal for offside, Zola took Costacurta's long pass wide of Sol Campbell to the right and shot powerfully inside Ian Walker's near post. It was the goal of a master. His first touch was perfect and the finish devastating. He had a similar chance, closer in, against Middlesbrough in the Cup Final,

but Ben Roberts stood up well and blocked it.

When Graham Rix signalled to him to make way for Gianluca Vialli two minutes from time, he smiled broadly. 'I thought that was magnificent,' Alan Hansen told BBC viewers.

FAR LEFT: Zola's delight is obvious after his superb goal in the FA Cup semi-final at Highbury, against Wimbledon, has ensured Chelsea's place in the final.

BELOW: As Ruud Gullit allows Luca Vialli a taste of FA Cup glory with two minutes to go at Wembley, Zola graciously makes way for his fellow countryman.

Roberto Di Matteo
samples the
delights of the
English tabloid
newspapers as he
relaxes at the
Chelsea training
ground in west
London.

Roberto Di Matteo was an unhappy man in the summer of 1996. Zdenek Zeman, the former Czech basketball coach who managed Di Matteo's club Lazio, was critical of him in the Italian press and it was apparent he no longer enjoyed his support. Di Matteo had just established himself as a midfield player in the Italian side, and his decision to take a day off after one game infuriated Zeman, who was renowned for demanding maximum physical effort from his players.

When an unforced error by Di Matteo against Inter led to an unpopular defeat, Zeman blamed him personally for the setback. Di Matteo announced he would have to leave and within hours Ruud Gullit was in contact, asking him whether he wanted to join Chelsea. Sergio Cragnotti, the Lazio president who brought Paul Gascoigne to Rome, was reluctant to sell Di Matteo but, realising he had little choice, accepted an offer of £4.9 million from Colin Hutchinson.

Di Matteo's departure angered some of the Lazio supporters and his taxi was spat on as it left Cragnotti's office following the completion of the deal. Earlier, the entry phone and post box of his home had been vandalised. A quiet, almost introspective man, Di Matteo found it hard to adapt to the volatile atmosphere of Roman football. He found he was recognised everywhere and often abused.

London was the complete opposite. After a brief spell in a hotel, the club found him a flat in Kensington and when he walked the streets, he was left unmolested. 'I enjoy the privacy and I enjoy London,' he said. 'But it has not been easy. My girlfriend did not want to live in London so I lived on my own. Now I know how to cook for myself, but I still have a cleaner to help me around the apartment.' There was a crisis for him on one occasion when he returned from an international match to discover that the water pipes in his flat had burst and the flat was flooded.

Like Zola, he believes playing in English football has enhanced his career. 'In Italy I was more of a defensive midfield player,' he said. 'Ruud has given me much greater freedom to go forward and score goals. If there is a possibility to score, then I go forward to try to take it. Scoring a goal fires my emotions. The crowd love goals.

'Ruud has given me more confidence and that is very important for me. Technically I do not think I have changed. My technique was good before I came. I think so, anyway.'

Di Matteo has an unusual background. He was born in Schaffhausen, in German Switzerland, the son of an immigrant worker from the Abruzzi, and spent most of his life in Switzerland.

He played for his local club as an 18-year-old before joining Zurich and later SC Aarau. The

ambition of his parents was for him to succeed with a *Serie A* club in Italy and they were overjoyed when he was signed by Lazio. His debut for Italy came in November 1994 and it was not a happy start, the *Azzurri* losing 2-1 at home to the emerging Croatian side. But manager Arrigo Sacchi kept faith in Di Matteo and he remained in the side.

For an Italian, Di Matteo has a peculiar temperament. He shows little emotion and has the calmness of an English infantryman under fire. His eyes will occasionally light up if someone says something funny, but his face is mainly expressionless. This feeling of being in control is carried onto the pitch. He will do the simple thing well, and consistently. His mistakes are few and he will rarely become involved in shouting matches with friend or foe. He exudes sureness and it is reassuring for the younger players to know he is there to pass to and help them out.

FAR LEFT: Di Matteo keeps a cool head as tempers flare, stepping in to keep his team-mate Frank Leboeuf out of trouble at the Baseball Ground in March 1997.

ABOVE: A change of direction and Di Matteo leaves Middlesbrough's Juninho for dead on his home League debut for the Blues. His second-half goal gave Chelsea a 1-0 victory.

Di Matteo exudes calmness, almost serenity, when in action (LEFT). But he also has a more aggressive side to his game, as he shows here (BELOW), coming in to make a block tackle on Tottenham's Sol Campbell.

Halfway through the season Gullit decided to drop him from the side. Surprisingly, the decision caused very little comment in the press. Di Matteo took it without complaint. 'Every player has a time when he needs to take a little time out and refresh himself,' Gullit explained. 'I think it did him good and I was pleased with the way he reacted.' Fortunately for Di Matteo, it did not harm his international prospects.

'I told him I did not see from him what I expected from him,' said Gullit. 'I just gave him a couple of weeks' good training and he relaxed himself. I think sometimes you have to protect the player from himself, give him the right boost to come back again.'

Interviewed on the pitch at Wembley before the FA Cup Final, Di Matteo admitted he was nervous. 'I couldn't sleep too well,' he said. But he was wide awake in the opening seconds when Dennis Wise won possession in the Middlesbrough half and passed to him. The Boro midfielders were not concentrating. Typically, Di Matteo was modest afterwards when he was accosted by the BBC's Ray Stubbs. 'I was confused,' he said. 'I just thought I should shoot and I was very lucky.' He had gone into the Cup Final record books as the scorer of the fastest goal at Wembley.

Like Zola, Di Matteo chose to live in the most exciting part of London, in a property overlooking Hyde Park near the Royal Albert Hall, Harrods and Harvey Nichols. Zola moved in nearby to a flat in Sloane Square. Di Matteo lived alone but often had members of his family staying with him. 'Football in Italy has changed,' he told one journalist. 'Older players say it has got worse. Every game, if you lose, it is like the end of the world. In England, pure sport still exists, pure football. If you give everything for ninety minutes and the opposition have been better, *si fa i complimenti*, fans understand this. It is not a cultural issue. It is the mentality that is different.'

What he also liked about English football was that the players were not required to spend the night before a home match together at a quiet hotel. 'This is a very positive thing in England,' he said. 'Players in Italy do not much like the *ritiro*, as it is called. We do not see it as a good thing for our work. There is no point to it. I am 27 and I felt this wish to go it alone. In England you have more responsibility. You become more autonomous, more mature. More of a man.'

Gianluca Vialli shaved his head, he said, 'because I wanted a change of luck. Until that luck runs out, my head will remain shaven.' Being signed by Chelsea and paid £1 million a year to be a part-time player is obviously considered by him to be lucky, because his hairstyle remained unaltered during his first season at Stamford Bridge. Living in the heart of London's Belgravia, which he adores, must also be considered lucky. But only two minutes of action in the FA Cup Final? Could that be classed as lucky? Yes, indeed!

'I was very happy that Chelsea won the FA Cup,' Vialli said. It brought him yet another medal to add to his two championship medals in Italy, three Italian Cup winners' medals and medals from all three European club competitions.

'I think the fans love me,' he said. 'The players love me. I am happy.' The players confirmed that. 'He's a lovely guy,' said Dennis Wise. Vialli kept their esteem because he never sulked when he was left out of the side. He just kept training harder than anyone, often staying out on the training pitch long after most of the others had gone in.

He has an unusual background. The youngest of five children of Gianfranco Vialli, a rich construction-firm owner, and his

Vialli shows his joy at scoring his first goal for Chelsea. He was the club's leading scorer for much of the season.

wife Marioli, Gianluca was born into opulent surroundings and has constructed his life accordingly ever since. He was small and weak as a young child but by the time he was thirteen had matured into a fine all-round sportsman capable of beating his older brothers at tennis, basketball and football. His motivation was never money, only the urge to work his body hard and to make the best use of his talents . . . and enjoy a pleasant life off the field.

His career was exceptional even by Italian standards. In 325 Serie A games for Cremonese, Sampdoria and Juventus, he scored 123 goals, and for Italy his tally was sixteen in 59 appearances. A few days before he signed for Chelsea on a free transfer, he lifted the European Cup as the Juventus captain following a tense penalty shoot-out against the holders Ajax. At 31, he was a sportsman at the very summit of his career.

Because of the Bosman ruling, no transfer fee was involved if he moved to another country and though several Italian clubs were interested, his choice lay between Chelsea and perpetual Scottish champions Glasgow Rangers. Chelsea's offer was £22,000 a week, a flat in London and a chauffeur-driven car. The offer from Rangers was greater in terms of monthly salary, but London swayed it for him. He wrote to David Murray, the Rangers chairman: 'As promised, I am telling you before anyone else about my decision. Until the last minute, Rangers was my first choice. The quality of life in Glasgow and my relationship with you are exceptional. But my dream to play in London prevails and as time passed by it gradually overcame everything. I feel I must accept the challenge before me but I sincerely hope I will meet you again soon.'

He explained: 'Glasgow is not London, so it had to be England for me. London is my dream. It is the greatest city in Europe, if not the world. I am looking forward to losing myself in London. In Italy you can go nowhere. You have to hide yourself away because of the fans.'

When he played at Sampdoria with Graeme Souness, he lived in an 18th-century villa overlooking the sea at Nervi, one of the most exclusive small towns along that part of the coast. Although he had several powerful cars, he often rode to the club's mountainside training ground on a Vespa. One of his coaches said of him: 'He is a genuine *capo carismatico*, a charismatic leader whose very state of mind profoundly affects his team-mates' performances.' Another coach said, 'He is much too nice on the pitch.'

His brother Nino was delighted Luca chose Chelsea because Nino is actually a Chelsea supporter himself. 'I watch their games on satellite TV wearing my blue-and-white scarf and shout for them to win,' he said.

Another attraction for the youngest of the Vialli family was that he would be playing for his former Sampdoria colleague Ruud Gullit. 'He asked me what I wanted out of life, sporting and non-sporting,' said Luca. 'After discussing things, he said to me: "Chelsea is the place for you, London has everything." Like me, Ruud is a winner. I feel like a kid going off to play in a completely new environment with new challenges.' Vialli's English at the time was sketchy, but he did

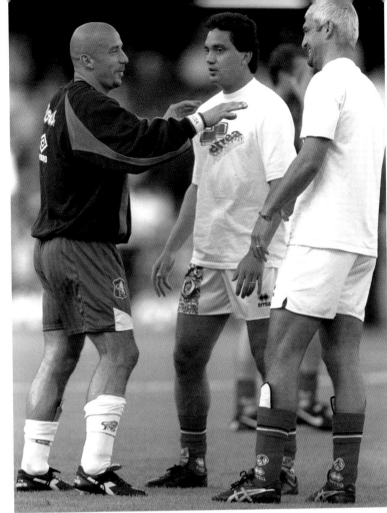

MAIN PICTURE: The famed Vialli overhead kick. Some of his most spectacular goals have come from variations of this particular skill.

RIGHT: Former Juventus team-mates Vialli and Ravanelli prepare to line up against each other as Middlesbrough visit Chelsea.

his best. It improved swiftly once he started regular lessons.

The crowd responded to him and his opening performances, though not dynamic, were encouraging. Then he was injured and when Zola arrived in November,

Vialli's luck appeared to be running out because Gullit decided that Mark Hughes and Zola were the best attacking partnership, with Zola having a free role on both sides of the pitch and Hughes the target man in the middle. There was no room in Gullit's tactical plan for all three of them, so Vialli was left out.

It must have hurt his pride, but he didn't show it. A player who had not long ago been on the winning

side in the European Cup Final could hardly be expected to play in the reserves, so it meant he was short of match practice. He made amends by training even harder.

Gullit was unconcerned about the situation because he knew that if Hughes or Zola was injured, he had an experienced, worldly-wise player to bring in. Hughes has rarely gone through a season without some kind of injury, because it is the way he plays. And most seasons he has also missed games through suspension.

Unfortunately for Vialli, whereas Hughes had gone over the 40-point disciplinary mark the previous season, this time he was suspended for only one match. And he performed so well that there was no question of him being omitted, even for tactical reasons. Zola, of course, could not be left out, so brilliantly was he playing. Only when Gullit decided to rest Zola for two matches before the Cup Final did Vialli return, other than in odd matches.

It was a curious existence for a man earning £1 million a year, almost like the head of a big company who only appears in the firm's main office a couple of days a month. He was enjoying the life of a gentleman footballer. A chauffeur-driven car of modest proportions took him around London. At night there were a host of restaurants, mainly Italian, available to entertain him and his friends. Colleagues revealed he sometimes spent £400 a time on taking them out. It was not debauchery, Gazza-style. Vialli hardly drank. It was good living in the style of a millionaire.

As the season wore on, stories started appearing in Italian newspapers about a supposed rift between Vialli and Gullit. They were quickly followed up by newspapers in England and there was even a suggestion that Gullit left his former friend out of the

THE BALD BRIGADE

Despite the high profile of Sir Bobby Charlton, there have been relatively few bald-headed footballers. In the main, they are a hirsute breed. Each generation had its outstanding examples of bald-headed players: Jimmy Goodall, one of Preston's Invincibles; Bill Shankly, Stan Cullis, Ron Burgess, Jimmy Melia, Howard Kendall and old 'Bald Eagle' himself, Jim Smith, among them.

Nowadays there appear to be more than ever and that is almost entirely due to the shaven-head look. And Chelsea, it seems, have more than most.

Gianluca Vialli and Frank Leboeuf may be receding but they do have plenty of hair left . . . except that they choose not to show it. Frank Sinclair, Eddie Newton, Andy Myers, Mark Stein and Dennis Wise have all joined the skinhead look. Two people most unlikely to follow the trend are, of course, Ruud Gullit and Gianfranco Zola.

side because he was jealous of his lifestyle. Matters reached a climax before the home game against Arsenal when Gullit said Vialli was 'a jinx on the team'. He explained: 'When he plays, we lose.' A fact that was trotted out was that Vialli had appeared in seven out of the eight matches Chelsea had lost up to that point in the season.

'He wants to prove those statistics wrong,' said Gullit.

'He feels 200 per cent and wants to prove a point to the crowd. They love him and I think he will be on top form for this one. I think he will be on fire.' If that was an attempt to gee Vialli up, it failed miserably because the next day Chelsea lost 3-0 to Arsenal in front of a stunned Bridge. Gullit was scathing. 'Any team in the four divisions would have beaten my side, the way they played today,' he said. 'For Arsenal it was

an exhibition game. My players should be ashamed. Only two, Jody Morris and Danny Granville, showed any passion. The others let themselves down. Our fans must have been astonished to see us play in that way.'

Ken Bates was not so upset. 'We had a mickey-mouse back three playing,' he said. Paul Parker, who was hired to cover for injuries, lasted only until half-time before he was substituted.

LEFT: For the most part, the 1996-97 season was a struggle for Vialli. Here he finds the going tough early on against Sheffield Wednesday at Hillsborough.

FAR LEFT: Heads down as Vialli battles for the ball with fellow skinhead Julian Dicks at Upton Park. In a rare outing, Vialli scored but the so-called 'jinx' struck again as Chelsea lost 3-2.

Vialli came in for some rough treatment in the newspapers and when he was told Gullit had criticised him (actually, Gullit had not named anyone, merely speaking of the players collectively) he was stung to reply: 'It is not unusual for the manager to criticise me. It does not matter if I do not play. Every time he plays me I will do my best for Chelsea. I am not a Chelsea problem.'

Within a few days the two men had a meeting and Gullit emerged to say there were no problems and Vialli would be staying. What he might have said was that at £1 million a year, no other club in England could afford Vialli's wages. Italian clubs were similarly ill-disposed towards bringing him home. At 32 he had only a limited future at the top level . . . and he was going to enjoy it.

When he returned home after the club's end-of-season tour to Brunei, Hong Kong and Bangkok, Vialli held an end-of-term dinner party for some of his team-mates in Soho. A lively evening ended with him being presented with a chocolate cake with the words 'Goodbye Luca from all the boys' iced on top.

Strangely, for someone who is extremely careful about what he eats and drinks, Vialli was a regular smoker. Smoking is a habit that has virtually died out in most English football clubs, but for all their addiction to physical fitness on the Continent, it remains part of their sporting culture. Most of the older breed of coaches in Europe can be seen puffing away. When a female writer from *Esquire* magazine asked Vialli

about this apparent breach of his fitness code, he protested: 'I don't smoke that much. Only occasionally.' And at the start of the 1997-98 season he announced he was giving up altogether.

He claimed not to be a heavy drinker either. 'A glass of two of wine at dinner is okay, but some people drink to alter their consciousness and then are no longer themselves. They become aggressive. The important thing if you are a footballer is not to get drunk. When I see someone getting drunk, it bothers me.'

Eating out regularly, he insisted, was no problem. 'I am not a slave to food,' he said. 'I am not a glutton.' While in London, he ate regularly at the San Lorenzo restaurant and, not carrying money with him, paid his bill monthly by credit card.

His views about the roughness of English football were no doubt reinforced by the way Di Matteo and Zola were treated by Stuart Pearce in the match between England and Italy during Le Tournoi in June 1997. 'I think English football is harder on an athletic level,' he said. 'Referees never seem to blow their whistles, so the whole game is harder. Every week, someone is hurt, someone breaks his leg or splits open his head. There is more fair play in Italy. No-one sets out to jeopardise another footballer's career. I played at Leeds in December and it was like playing rugby.' Chelsea lost that match 2-0 and a 3-0 defeat in the next away match at Sunderland was equally annoying for Gullit. It proved that some of his players were reluctant to stand up to intimidation.

AIER LEAC

Frank and Bette Leboeuf live five minutes from Stamford Bridge. Pride of place in their home goes to an antique chair which is upholstered in the blue shirt which Frank wore on his international debut on August 16, 1995. It says a lot about him, and his wife. He is a man who has great pride in his work and Bette, an attractive young woman with a model's figure, wants to see that his achievements are remembered. It is a skilful piece of millinery, for even the collar is preserved. On the back of the chair is the number five.

Some critics said he was too slow, too old and not a good enough defender to play international football when he made his debut. With his receding hair, he looks older than his 28 years. Too slow? 'I will leave that to the English public to decide,' said Leboeuf. He is a thinking footballer. He senses

'In France a defender cannot touch a forward. If you do, the referee will blow his whistle. Here you have to battle.'

the threat early and if you do that, there is less call to be lightning fast. There have been isolated occasions when his defensive

qualities may have let him down, but not many.

Where there was some doubt about him concerned his ability to counter the hurly-burly of the English game and it surfaced at the home game against Wimbledon in October 1996 which Chelsea lost 4-2. The Wimbledon strikers set out to unnerve him with their aggression and he took some punishing blows. It was a salutary experience for him. By the time the two teams met again, he had erased all doubts. Physically he was their match.

Oddly, he claims he likes the combative nature of English football. 'In France a defender cannot touch a forward,' he says. 'You cannot go to battle with him because if you do, every time the referee will blow his whistle. Here you have to battle.'

ABOVE: Leboeuf shows the quality of his tackling in this sequence as he dispossesses Newcastle's Tino Asprilla. When he arrived Frank was criticised for not being physical enough. He soon answered his critics.

PREVIOUS PAGE: He's here, he's there . . . and on this occasion, to the delight of the fans behind the North Stand goal, Frank Leboeuf was in the Aston Villa penalty area to score Chelsea's equaliser in a 1-1 draw.

Other sides have tried to rough him up because they recognise there are some times when he is Chelsea's best attacking player, a sweeper who performs the role of a quarterback in the side, finding space and then delivering thirty or forty-yard balls to the forwards. 'I have played this position now for ten years and for me it is the most important position of all,' said Leboeuf. 'I can determine how Chelsea play the game.'

When Ruud Gullit first came to Chelsea, he played in that role. Glenn Hoddle saw Gullit as the ideal person there, mainly because of the infinite range of his long passing. Gullit knew that he was not a good enough defender to continue in the role, so after taking over as manager he started negotiations with Leboeuf and his father, who was Frank's agent. Leboeuf junior was playing for Strasbourg at the time and the clubs quickly agreed a fee of £2.5 million. There was an offer from Marseille, the nearest club to St Cyr where Frank was born, but he preferred Chelsea despite not having been to England before.

His father played professionally for Reims and was responsible for training him when he was a youth. Frank's first club was Toulon, where he shared a room with David Ginola, but at 18 he was sacked. He took a job as a travelling salesman and continued playing in local football as an amateur. His breakthrough came when he sent a video of himself to two First Division clubs, Laval and Auxerre, and Laval signed him. He had three seasons with them before joining Strasbourg, where he stayed for two years.

TOP LEFT: Leboeuf takes the ball off Portsmouth's Paul Hall during the FA Cup quarter-final at Fratton Park.

LEFT: He puts in a challenge to deny Rory Allen of Spurs during what Chelsea fans have come to regard as their annual victory at White Hart Lane.

ABOVE: Marching out at Wembley on Cup Final day, a proud moment for a determined Frank Leboeuf.

After the pre-season victory over Sampdoria in 1996, Dennis Wise said to his new team-mate: 'I think we are going to surprise a few people this year.'

'I had to agree with him,' said Leboeuf. 'We came together very quickly because we had so many intelligent players. Everyone made the effort to blend in. There are tremendous qualities in the team and I believe we can still improve. I know I have not achieved yet what I want to bring to this team.

'The general feeling is that this club is buzzing, that this is the place where it is happening. I love playing in England. It is an extraordinary experience, the atmosphere in the stadium, the city, everything. And I find the people are so courteous. Especially on the road. Try to cross the street in Paris and you play with your life!'

His interest in London and its attractions is apparent to everyone who meets him. He wants to be part of the culture as much as the football, and that is undoubtedly one of the reasons why he and the other foreign players have acclimatised so quickly. His English, good when he arrived, has also improved.

Many English players have failed to establish themselves abroad because they were unable to learn the language quickly enough and showed little or no interest in their new environment. They kept themselves cooped up in their expensive houses and flats. Those who did prosper, like Joe Jordan and Ray Wilkins in Milan, learned Italian and adopted an Italian style of life.

The Leboeuf household is full of souvenirs and bric-a-brac including Gaugin prints, gilt mirrors, art nouveau pieces and a porcelain football boot. There is also a policeman's helmet on display. In short, they are rounded, intelligent young people.

Leboeuf takes a breather in the changing-room after training: 'The general feeling is that this club is buzzing.'

PLAYER	COUNTRY	PREVIOUS CLUB	DATE SIGNED	FEE
Dmitri Kharine	Russia	CSKA Moscow	Dec 1992	£200,000
Ruud Gullit	Holland	Sampdoria	May 1995	FREE
Dan Petrescu	Romania	Sheffield Wednesday	Nov 1995	£2.3m
Frank Leboeuf	France	Strasbourg	Jun 1996	£2.5m
Gianluca Vialli	Italy	Juventus	Jun 1996	FREE
Roberto Di Matteo	Italy	Lazio	Jul 1996	£4.9m
Gianfranco Zola	Italy	Parma	Nov 1996	£4.5m
Frode Grodas	Norway	Lillestrom	Nov 1996	FREE
Celestine Babayaro	Nigeria	Anderlecht	May 1997	£2m
Ed de Goey	Holland	Feyenoord	Jun 1997	£2.25m
Gustavo Poyet	Uruguay	Real Zaragoza	Jun 1997	FREE
Bernard Lambourde	France	Bordeaux	Jun 1997	£1.5m
Tore Andre Flo	Norway	Brann Bergen	Jul 1997	£300,000

According to the former Chelsea manager Dave Sexton, the Romanian Dan Petrescu is the outstanding right-side wing back in the world. He may well be right. Petrescu was playing in the position before most coaches had heard of it. He hasn't had the attention and the publicity of the Italian imports, but in many ways he has been just as effective. There is a wealth of experience in the way he plays, the way he wins the ball with well-timed tackles and uses it with measured, accurate passes.

Undemonstrative as a person, he is equally undemonstrative on the field. When he left Bucharest following the downfall of the Communist regime, he had a spell with Genoa, the Italian club, before David Pleat took him to Sheffield Wednesday for £1.25 million. When Chelsea tried to buy him the following season, there were problems over a lingering

knee injury and it was some weeks before the £2.3 million deal was completed. His second season at the Bridge saw him develop into an integral part of Gullit's plan to put the club on the same standing as the top clubs in Europe, and his performance in the FA Cup Final was hugely influential. Gullit employed him in that match as an attacking midfield player on the right and it suited him.

Russian keeper Dmitri Kharine, on the other hand, had a year to forget. In the fifth game of the season at Sheffield Wednesday, he damaged his knee and the cruciate ligaments snapped, a rare injury for a goalkeeper. He spent lonely months in rehabilitation and only towards the end of the season was he able to start light training. When his deputy Kevin Hitchcock was also injured, Gullit had scouts scouring Europe for a suitable stand-in. German goalkeeper Georg Koch of Fortuna Dusseldorf might have been the man but

Fortuna wanted too much at £2 million. Instead, Gullit took the Norwegian number one Frode Grodas on loan for £60,000 from Lillestrom and subsequently signed him on a free transfer. Grodas proved somewhat idiosyncratic, sound with his positioning so that he was often able to make goalsaving blocks, but prone to bewildering errors, like the last-minute fumble which presented Sheffield Wednesday with a point at the Bridge.

'I made mistakes,' Grodas admitted in good English, 'but all keepers do that. David James has made them but he is still one of the top three in England. There is a thin dividing-line between being a hero and a clown.'

'When I came to England I expected to be number one and I did not come to sit on the bench. I have been an international since 1991.'

Grodas and the other three goalkeepers on the staff must have been disheartened when they read on June 12, 1997 that the Dutch international Ed de Goey had been signed from Feyenoord for £2.25 million. De Goey, 30, signed a five-year contract.

'This is a dream move,' he said. 'Several Dutch and Spanish clubs have shown an interest in me, but when I knew that Ruud wanted me, there was only one club for me – Chelsea. The prospect of

LEFT: Signed by Glenn Hoddle, Dan Petrescu is the world's best wing-back, says another former Chelsea boss, Dave Sexton.

ABOVE: Dutch international goalkeeper Ed de Goey was a welcome arrival at Stamford Bridge in the summer of 1997.

playing in England with a big club like Chelsea really excites me.'

In all, Gullit brought five more foreigners to Stamford Bridge during the 1997 close season, enabling him to field an all-foreign side if he wished. As well as De Goey there was Celestine Babayaro, the left-sided 19-year-old Nigerian international from Anderlecht; Gustavo Poyet, the Uruguayan midfielder from Real Zaragoza; defender Bernard Lambourde from Bordeaux; and the Norwegian striker Tore Andre Flo. According to experts in Norway, he has the potential and determination to emerge as the best of a crop of exciting young strikers from Scandinavia.

GWYN WILLIAMS, CHELSEA'S NURSEMAID TO THE STARS

Welshman Gwyn Williams was a deputy headmaster in 1979 when he saw an advertisement saying that Chelsea Football Club wanted a youth development officer. He had never played professional football at a high level, only non-League football for Wimbledon and Kingstonian. But Geoff Hurst, who was Chelsea's manager at the time, was impressed with his credentials and enthusiasm and Williams has been at the club ever since as youth team coach, reserve coach, chief scout, general manager and now chief administrative officer.

One of his main tasks is to look after the foreign players when they arrive and find accommodation for them. It can be a wearisome task, especially if the player speaks no English. When Russian goalkeeper Dmitri Kharine arrived, there were special problems. Kharine showed no aptitude for picking up the language quickly and Williams had to take a Russian-English dictionary to meetings with him. After six weeks in a hotel, Kharine was eventually fixed up with a house on Christmas Eve.

He went out shopping with his wife and when he returned he found the house had been broken into and all his cash – a considerable sum of US dollars – and most valuable possessions had been stolen. 'It's Christmas, he's 3,000 miles from home, doesn't know anyone, can't speak a word of English and suddenly he needs a new front door - you can imagine the shock,' said Williams.

'We managed to sort it out and he's done very well except that he missed most of the 1996-97 season after damaging the cruciate ligaments in his knee. It's been a very frustrating time for him.'

Williams also has to find schools for the children of the stars. Most of them are appreciative of his efforts but there have been other players with problems which have proved more difficult to solve.

'Franco was great,' he said. 'It couldn't have gone better. He knew exactly what he wanted and within ten days he and his family had moved into a house. He even organised his own English lessons. Luca was a bit different. He's a single man and it took ages to find somewhere that suited him. The problem was that people knew he had a lot of money and kept asking for more than things were worth.

'The main thing is that these guys are top players and top timekeepers and trainers. They've been a good influence in many ways. For instance, ten years ago on the way back from somewhere like Newcastle, it would be nothing for players to drink six pints of ale. Now it's all soft drinks and water and no-one thinks about it.'

Gwyn has worked under eight managers at Chelsea: Hurst, John Neal, John Hollins, Bobby Campbell, Ian Porterfield, David Webb, Glenn Hoddle and now Ruud Gullit. 'No two have been the same but the big change came when Glenn arrived. He looked after everything. Ruud is great to work with, not afraid to make difficult decisions, but I've never once heard him raise his voice.'

Besides all his other duties, Williams spends a lot of time acting as a scout at matches. It often means an eighteen-hour day. And there are few days off for him in the season.

Nor are there many for the personnel manager Denise Summers, who does a lot of the day-to-day work. Before the 1996 club Christmas party, the Kharine family said they would not be able to come. Denise discovered that their five-year-old son Igor had been told that he had to stand up and tell a story, and the prospect terrified him. So she penned a letter to Igor signed 'Father Christmas' saying that he did not have to read a story.

The Kharines duly turned up.

RIGHT: Chelsea's Mr Fix-It, Gwyn Williams (right), on the pitch with Erland Johnsen at Wembley before the Cup Final. One of Williams' major responsibilities is to ease the foreign players into the English way of life. Here, however, the pair are sorting out Erland's Cup Final tickets!

THE HOME GUARD

CUTTING OUT THE CHASE

Ruud Gullit has simple, but firm, ideas about the game and Mark Hughes testifies how Gullit changed his style and made him a better player at the age of 32. 'When I played for Manchester United I spent a lot of time running about, chasing full-backs down and tackling midfield players,' he said. 'That was all well and good, I was doing my job for the side, but it took something away from my game as an attacking player. I would be too tired to get into the box. I had expended my energies in other areas, areas where I wasn't hurting teams.

'This season Rudi said very early on that he doesn't want his strikers chasing after full-backs. He wants them fresh for when they are trying to get into the box. It has taken me fifteen years to realise I have been playing the game the wrong way!'

Getting forwards to chase back and defend has long been a part of English football, and it grew out of the fear of losing. Managers would praise their strikers for their defensive qualities. Not this one. 'I want my forwards to score goals, not waste their energy tackling opponents,' explained Gullit. 'The crucial time for them is when they have a chance to score. If they are ready for it and not tired through running about too much, they have a better chance of making a goal.' The 'new' Mark Hughes scored five times in the 1997 FA Cup run to help Chelsea reach Wembley.

The day Ruud Gullit was confirmed as having signed for the club, Chelsea also announced that they had signed Mark Hughes from Manchester United for £1.5 million. In some quarters it was not seen as a forward-looking move because Hughes was 31 at the time and his striking rate was on the decline after years of punishment as a target player – a target not only for the passes of his colleagues but also for the kicks, shoves and nudges of his opponents.

'He's like a relic from the Stone Age,' said Gullit. 'He has such strength.' The circumference of Hughes's thighs measures 25 inches, as much as a heavyweight boxer, and his ankles are also much bigger than the average footballer's. Strong legs, strong heart, he felt he was ready for a few more years in the Premiership and so it proved. He became one of the mainstays of the Home Guard, the players from the British Isles responsible for the brickwork while the foreigners slapped on the gloss.

At Manchester United, Hughes won all the honours going in the English game before he realised that his manager Alex Ferguson was no longer one of his most ardent supporters. 'It was time to move on,' he said. 'They didn't want me to stay.' He had never

LEFT: Hughes uses his great body strength to shield the ball from Newcastle United's Philippe Albert and David Batty during the 1-1 draw at Stamford Bridge.

ABOVE: Despite his comparative lack of height, Hughes wins the ball in the air more than most taller strikers. Here he does it again against West Ham.

relished all the attention. A quiet, almost shy person, he was a reluctant interviewee. When his work was over, he was off to his wife and three children in their Cheshire home.

He had joined United from school where he developed a rewarding relationship with one of his headmasters, Harold Potter, in his native Ruabon, near Wrexham. When Potter contracted the dreaded Alzheimer's Disease,

Mark visited him regularly and his grief was hugely apparent when he attended the funeral. He once said: 'I like my own company. When I get onto the field, I have always found I can express myself a lot better than I can off it.'

In his first season with Chelsea Hughes scored eight goals in 31 appearances in the Premiership plus four in the FA Cup, making him the side's second top scorer behind John Spencer, the Scot

who was sold to QPR for £2.5 million and in turn became their highest scorer. The proud Spencer had not been prepared to wait for a regular place and, along with Gavin Peacock, another fine servant of the club, he was packed off up the road to Shepherd's Bush. Both players profited from the deal in terms of personal achievement even if they were now performing in the Nationwide First Division.

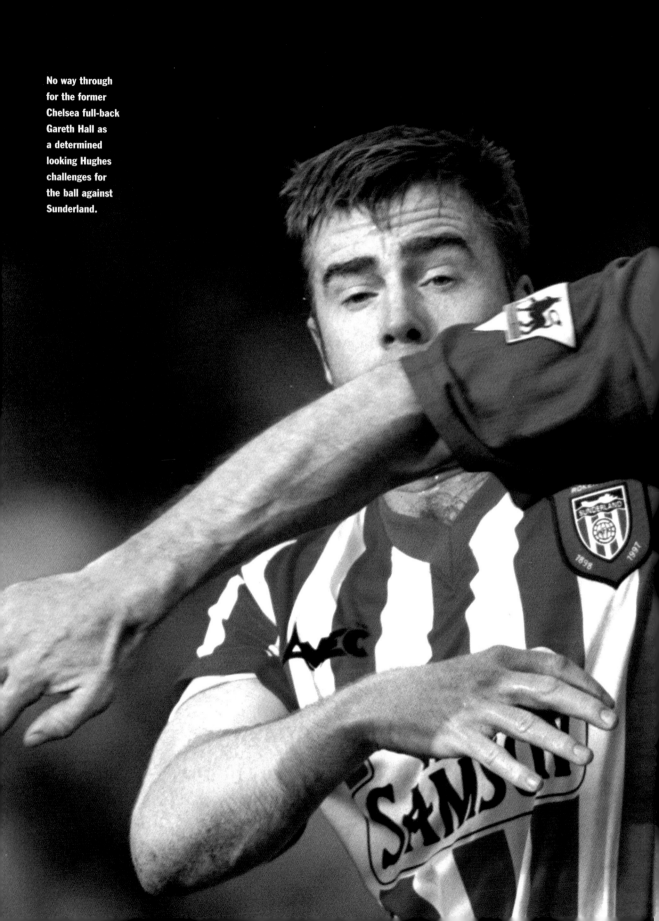

No way through
for the former
Chelsea full-back
Gareth Hall as
a determined
looking Hughes
challenges for
the ball against
Sunderland.

Gullit saw Hughes as such a vital part of his team plans that he was prepared to let him continue living in Cheshire. Hughes had an arrangement with British Airways enabling him to have a cut-price season ticket on the Manchester-Heathrow shuttle and the club found him a flat on the Mill Ride Golf Course for the days when he was required to stay overnight. At the end of the 1996-97 season, there were hints in some newspapers that these arrangements were unsatisfactory and Hughes wanted to return to the North. Gullit himself fuelled them by saying: 'He lives a long way away and we have to sit down and talk about things.'

In the week of the FA Cup Final, Mark's agent Dennis Roach agreed an extension to his contract for a further two years, which ended

THE MEDALS OF MARK HUGHES

WITH MANCHESTER UNITED

Premier League	1992-93	1993-94	
FA Cup	1985	1990	1994
League Cup	1992		
FA Charity Shield	1993		
European Cup-Winners' Cup	1991		
European Super Cup	1991		

WITH CHELSEA

FA Cup	1997

the speculation. 'I'm very pleased to be staying,' said Hughes. 'I want to continue being a regular in the side but if I don't play as many games as I think I should play, I don't think it would be as much of a problem as it might have been a few years ago. Having said that, I have no intention of winding down. I feel as fit and as enthusiastic as ever and I will keep going as long as possible.'

Footballer of the Year in the PFA ballot in 1989 and 1991, Hughes came close again in 1997. The catalyst for his season, perhaps even for the club, came in that marvellous FA Cup fourth round tie against Liverpool on January 26 when he was relegated to the substitutes' bench at the start. Liverpool were in such domineering form that they led 2-0 at half-time. Gullit realised he needed Hughes out there and when he sent him on for Scott Minto at the start of the second half, Hughes responded by scoring in a minute. It was the defining moment of one of Chelsea's best performances for a long time.

Two goals from Vialli and one from Zola, and Hughes was back on course for his fourth FA Cup winners' medal, which he was to receive from the Duchess of Kent just over three months later.

His performance in the 1997 Cup Final was not one of his better ones, as he admitted. His success rate with passes, 63 per cent, was the lowest in the team, and he conceded nine of the 23 free-kicks Chelsea gave away, the next highest being the three of Frank Sinclair.

At Old Trafford Hughes was known as 'Sparky' because of the way he would lose his temper with opponents and referees. His disciplinary record there was a poor one, and it was not much better in his first season at Stamford Bridge as he picked up 45 disciplinary points.

There was a significant change-around in his second season at Chelsea. His approach showed greater signs of maturity and he missed only one match through suspension. His nickname was no longer 'Sparky' but – courtesy of Dennis Wise – 'Nigel', after the curly-haired character on television's *Eastenders*.

Frank Sinclair was another player who, like Mark Hughes, was offered a contract to stay after the 1996-97 season ended. There was speculation that QPR were after him, but Gullit wanted Sinclair to be part of his plans and the 25-year-old defender, who joined the club as a boy, had no wish to leave. He was one of Chelsea's most effective players in the FA Cup Final, playing out of position on the right and winning more tackles than anyone. He had not been a regular and only got his place back in January when Michael Duberry was put out of the game with his cruel Achilles tendon injury.

In many ways Sinclair resembles David Webb, a powerful jumper, a strong character and a man who is unlikely to quake after making mistakes. Players with these qualities are needed in any side to balance up with the Zolas, Viallis and Leboeufs.

Another player essential in a similar balancing role, in midfield, is Eddie Newton whose season had also been truncated, but by injury. In February the previous season, 1995-96, he broke his shinbone in a collision with Kevin Hitchcock, and when he returned, he tore a groin muscle. When Roberto Di Matteo arrived, Newton wondered whether he had a future at the club despite all the proclamations about how highly he was valued.

'Rob was playing in the holding role for Italy at the time and little doubts were going through my mind,' he admitted. But Gullit had more expansive plans for Di Matteo: he wanted him to concentrate more on the attacking side of his game, making more runs with the ball. Few midfield players in the Premiership have the skill or the confidence to run at defenders. Di Matteo has both. It meant that Newton was able to continue as the anchor man. He had been an attacking midfielder himself until Glenn Hoddle, noticing his skill at hustling opponents and winning tackles, changed him over. 'It is a role which is appreciated in the game but not so much by connoisseurs,' he said. 'Glenn said to me that he didn't think I was excellent at one thing but good at a lot of things and that was the position he wanted me to play in.'

NEWTON'S REWARD

A succession of managers and coaches have praised the otherwise unsung abilities of Eddie Newton, but it was not until Ruud Gullit explained why he would not be bidding for Paul Ince, as was being speculated upon in some newspapers, that everyone realised just how important a player Newton is at Stamford Bridge.

'I already have a player who plays in that area in the same role [as Ince] and I am very happy with him,' said Gullit. 'He is not one of the flair players, but he makes those players play.'

Brought up in Hammersmith as a QPR supporter, Newton joined the club as a 12-year-old at the same time as his closest friend Frank Sinclair, who is ten days older.

Eddie was 40–1 with the bookmakers to score the first goal at Wembley, principally because he hadn't scored a goal since November 1995. In the event he got Chelsea's second, and it was a fitting reward for someone who had fought back bravely after crippling injuries.

Newton was largely successful in stopping Eric Cantona in the 1994 Cup Final until he brought Dennis Irwin down early in the second half and gave away the penalty which put United on the way to a 4-0 victory. 'For the first hour we were running the game,' he said. 'The penalties killed us and that was it. That was one of the reasons why I was so pleased to score the second goal in the 1997 Final.'

ABOVE: Frank Sinclair bores through the challenges of West Ham's Marc Rieper (right) and Michael Hughes.

LEFT: Frank Leboeuf is down but Eddie Newton continues the attempt to foil Juninho in the FA Cup Final.

Ruud Gullit's most influential decision in the 1996-97 season was to drop skipper Dennis Wise, for so long a linchpin in the Chelsea side. 'Best thing he did,' said an admiring Ken Bates. 'It showed the others no-one was safe. Wisey was playing rubbish.' The skipper was soon back with an improved attitude and his game simplified. And like Mark Hughes, his disciplinary record was better. 'You can't win matches sitting in the stand suspended,' the manager told them.

Any successful sporting group needs a mix of stars, enthusiasts and those who will never let anyone down. Chelsea have been lucky over the past ten years to have Steve Clarke as the Old Reliable. Asked to name his chief asset, he replied: 'Consistency.' No Chelsea fan will argue with that. Even when he has been dropped, he has never really had a nightmare of a game. It has usually been because the manager of the day wanted to change things around. He has had six to contend with in his time: John Hollins, who was in charge when he arrived from St Mirren in January 1987 for a modest £422,000 fee; Bobby Campbell, who dropped him, a decision which led to an ill-timed transfer request; Ian Porterfield, David Webb, Glenn Hoddle and Ruud Gullit.

Steve Clarke was fortunate to survive childhood. When he was a young boy, an inflatable boat he was playing with drifted out to sea and was half a mile offshore before his father, an industrial chemist, noticed his predicament.

The skipper was soon back with an improved attitude... And his disciplinary record was better.

Fortunately, his father was a powerful swimmer and was able to drag him back to land. His first memory of seeing footballers in

action at the highest level was being present at the England v Scotland match at Wembley in 1967 as a four-year-old when the Scots won 3-2. The sight of seeing 'Slim Jim' Baxter and Denis Law in action fired an ambition which was to be realised when he signed for St Mirren. Quiet and determined, 30-year-old Clarke has been a role-model professional and he thoroughly deserved his testimonial.

Injuries during the season forced him to have a variety of partners ranging from Erland Johnsen, the likeable Norwegian who went home to Norway to continue his career outside the game, Frank Leboeuf and the unlucky Michael Duberry, to Frank Sinclair and the ill-fated Paul Parker. Left-back, too, was an unsettled position with Scott Minto vying for the job along with Sinclair and Andy Myers. Out of contract at the end of the season, Minto eventually signed for Benfica. Gullit filled the gap just before the start of the new season by bringing Graeme Le Saux home to Chelsea.

ABOVE: Mark Nicholls, a fine home-grown prospect, in action at the 1997 Umbro Cup tournament at Goodison Park. Chelsea beat Everton 3-1 in the final to win the trophy again.

RIGHT: Finding it difficult to claim a regular place in the Chelsea side, midfielder Craig Burley took the opportunity to join Celtic at the start of the 1997-98 season.

In goal, Kevin Hitchcock stood in for the injured Dmitri Kharine only to be forced out himself through an arm injury. The popular Frode Grodas came in, and when the young Irishman Nicky Colgan was called upon, he never let anyone down. But the fact remains Chelsea do not have a goalkeeper in the class of Peter Bonetti and Gullit is banking on Dutchman Ed de Goey to provide the necessary class.

The back-up in midfield held out the promise of players from this country coming through and saving the club from having to pay exorbitant wages to foreigners. In Jody Morris, the club have a young man with the passing potential of an Alan Hudson, and 21-year-old Paul Hughes also showed signs of being a clever, all-round midfield prospect. Mark Nicholls also made a handful of appearances for the first team in 1996-97, as did Danny Granville, a left-back.

The more experienced Craig Burley was understandably upset at being left out of the Cup Final line-up and it was an equally frustrating time for the other forgotten squad members, David Rocastle, Mark Stein and the injured David Lee. One or two may be back, but Burley, a Scot, was sold to Celtic. Nobody, and nothing, is permanent in a football club.

KEEPING CHELSEA FIT: ADE MAFE

One of Ruud Gullit's most important yet unheralded signings was the recruitment of the former Olympic sprinter Ade Mafe as the club's fitness trainer. In Europe fitness trainers have been an established part of the game for many years. They prepare the players before training, conducting stretching exercises and other routines, work with them during the initial part of the session and finish off afterwards with warm-downs.

Up until a few years ago, most English clubs let the physiotherapist handle these matters, if indeed they were felt necessary at all. At some clubs the players just went out and trained. They did a few laps to warm up and then underwent practice routines, finishing with a short-sided game. It might have yielded a few laughs, but it was a sign of how far English clubs lagged behind.

Gullit was determined to start off the Continental way. Someone recommended 30-year-old Mafe, who was a qualified masseur running his own fitness centre.

'I'd only been to see one football match before I joined Chelsea,' said Mafe. 'I found there were many things I could adapt to a football environment. All the players were in pretty good shape, although the foreign lads had a better mentality towards fitness conditioning because of their upbringing. They know that conditioning is as important as technical ability. Telling them to do something is not a problem. The British tend to think that if they can play football, they're okay. To get them to run is something you have to educate them about.'

Mafe sits on the bench assessing the performance levels of the players. 'If I see someone is flagging, I make a note and maybe give him a bit extra to do the following week,' he told Russell Kempson of The Times. 'I might say to Ruud "He's had it, he's knackered" and it is up to him whether he keeps the player on or takes him off.'

When Gullit injured his ankle, Mafe had to treat him like any other player. 'I had to push him,' he said. 'I couldn't be too soft on him. He tried to shirk it sometimes and moaned a bit, but he knew it was for his own benefit! He might be my boss but he is still a player and I told him to get on with it.'

Mafe, who was the youngest British male athlete to reach an Olympic final, has a two-year contract with Chelsea. He is popular with the players and they respect him and his background.

LEFT: Gianluca Vialli and Eddie Newton (right) are put through their warm-up routine by Ade Mafe (centre) on the pitch at Wembley before the FA Cup Final.

THE DI MATTEO CUP FINAL

A DOUBLE WINNER

The Wednesday before the FA Cup Final, Dennis Wise helped out with drawing the numbers for the National Lottery on television. Theresa Coneely, one of the club's longest-serving backroom staff, was one of the winners.

'It was only £10, but Dennis and Steve Clarke both told me to back Chelsea to win 2-0, which I did,' she said.

Bookmakers William Hill made Chelsea 2-1 on favourites to win the Cup and, for the first time ever, offered odds about the nationality of the first goalscorer. Not surprisingly, Italian was the favourite at 2-1, which proved correct. For the time of the first goal, however, Hills made 31-40 and 41-50 minutes joint favourites . . .

RIGHT: Up for the Cup! All the tension, colour and excitement of Cup Final day shows in the face of this Chelsea fan.

ABOVE RIGHT: Steve Clarke (centre of picture) in reflective mood as the players get a feel of the Wembley pitch.

FAR RIGHT: The skipper is dressed for the occasion, as (OVERLEAF) are Gianfranco Zola (left) and Frank Leboeuf.

Alan Hansen said it was 'a decent' FA Cup Final. That was probably a slight exaggeration. It was half-decent. But the 40,000 Chelsea supporters, just over half of whom were at Wembley, were not bothered about the quality of the game, only the result. Next day, the Blue Army had swelled to 60,000 as the ceremonial parade took place. Police tried, unavailingly, to break up night-long celebrations and one resident said: 'I didn't get a wink of sleep and I don't think many of my neighbours did either.'

With typical underplay, Ken Bates said: 'This has been the greatest party in the history of English football. This is the carnival cup, the happiest cup.' He was right about the happiness it brought. The after-match antics at Wembley were more exotic than any seen there before and the players stayed on the pitch longer than any previous winners. Jimmy Hill said: 'There is a real sense of joy and happiness out there. It's great for the game.'

Chelsea's 2-0 victory - like the lifting of a siege - came at a time when the nation was in the mood for good news. There was a feeling of expectancy among the people after the change of Government and they were ready to applaud

Chelsea supporters were not bothered about the quality of the game, only the result.

new heroes like Gianfranco Zola and Roberto Di Matteo who had smiles on their faces, not scowls like the departing hero of Old Trafford who announced his retirement the day after the Final.

Ruud Gullit was smiling when the teams emerged from the Wembley tunnel and was still smiling hours afterwards. 'I am really proud of this day,' he said. 'I feel I have grown up as a person. It is a great day, a great year and it went very fast.'

Throughout the build-up to the Final, Gullit had insisted that everything had to be done his way. He co-operated with the media but when the BBC, who had paid money into the players' pool, asked for permission to film on the coach taking the team from their hotel to Wembley, Gullit baulked. He wanted that period for quiet reflection.

When he announced the line-up to his players at 12.30, there was just one surprise - the formation would be 4-4-2 not 5-3-2, with Frank Sinclair at right-back and Dan Petrescu playing in an orthodox right-side midfield position. The idea was to press the play and deny Juninho space to run into and exploit. It worked. Middlesbrough's forwards were caught offside sixteen times, more than three times the average in a modern game. One of the worst

LEFT: The players are taken through a pre-match warm-up on the Wembley pitch by their fitness trainer Ade Mafe (third from right).

ABOVE: A proud manager, Ruud Gullit leads out his team. Some of them appear nervous but all are looking very determined.

offenders, until he went off after stretching his left hamstring again, was Fabrizio Ravanelli. In retrospect, Ravanelli ought not to have played, but he persuaded Bryan Robson to give him a chance and it was a costly error.

When Robbie Mustoe twisted his knee and retired five minutes later, it brought back memories of the Stanley Matthews Final when

Bolton had two players injured early on and were forced to play on with them because there were no substitutes in those days. It was cruel luck on Boro and further confirmation of the adage in football that if your luck is out, things will continue to go against you.

Robson brought central defender Steve Vickers in to partner the

admirable Nigel Pearson, and moved Gianluca Festa, another of Boro's few successes, into midfield. Robson might have erred by not having another striker on the bench to partner Ravanelli's replacement, the Dane Mikkel Beck, and there was criticism later of his failure to push Juninho, or anyone, further upfield in the closing stages.

Grodas

Sinclair

Leboeuf

Clarke

Minto

Petrescu

Newton

Di Matteo

Wise

Hughes

Zola

MIDDLESBROUGH

Roberts

Blackmore   **Festa**   **Pearson**   **Fleming**

Hignett (Kinder 74)   **Emerson**   **Mustoe** (Vickers 29)   **Stamp**

Ravanelli (Beck 24)   **Juninho**

CHELSEA SUBSTITUTES

Hitchcock

Myers

Vialli (for Zola 89)

A good indicator of what kind of Final it is going to be is the look in the eyes of the players as they stride up the tunnel from the cramped, 1920s-style dressing-rooms. Dennis Wise was smiling, along with Gullit, but most of the others appeared distinctly nervous, particularly Zola. Middlesbrough's players looked even more solemn. It was not a good portent. In past times the Final was the showpiece of the season and teams could afford to be more cavalier. In recent years it has become a stepping stone into European competition and clubs are more cautious. There is much more at stake. It is no longer just a Final, the climax to the season, but a qualifier for another tournament.

The nerves also seemed to have affected the new FA chairman Keith Wiseman. As the teams lined up for the presentation to the Duchess of Kent, he marched out to shake hands with Robson and turned to introduce the Duchess. He had forgotten that the National Anthem, or part of it, had to be played first.

The FA dignitaries found themselves being booed and jeered by the Middlesbrough supporters. Their club had had three League points deducted after pulling out of a game at Blackburn in December, and the punishment ended up costing them their Premiership place.

LEFT: Zola has a few words for Juninho (left) as possibly the two outstanding players of the season walk out side by side.

BELOW: Skipper Dennis Wise exchanges pennants with his opposite number Nigel Pearson of Middlesbrough.

OVERLEAF: Carefree, wherever they may be! The Chelsea end in full cry at Wembley.

The Boro fans were obviously under the mistaken impression that 'the FA' were the people who had deducted their three points. In fact, that decision was taken by an FA Premiership disciplinary panel and the FA appeals board turned down Middlesbrough's appeal. A coy Steve Gibson, the Boro chairman, refused to answer Des Lynam's questions on television about whether his club would take the matter to the High Court, or a European Court. 'You will learn of our intentions later,' he said.

Most finals are known for one moment and this one will go down as 'the final with the quickest ever goal at Wembley'. In just over half a minute, Wise won possession from Mustoe on the left, twenty yards inside his own half, and advanced a few yards crossfield towards the middle. He passed to the unmarked Di Matteo, who was approaching the centre circle in a central position. The crowd gasped. There was no Middlesbrough player in front of Di Matteo except Festa and he was busy marking Mark Hughes, who moved one way, then the other, to take the Italian out of range of Di Matteo.

Park teams rarely make mistakes as elementary as this – the demoted Premiership club had been caught out with none of its midfield players in a position to challenge Di Matteo. Emerson, roundly abused both from the terraces and from the BBC box, tried to make up some ground, but pace is not one of his attributes.

Zola sprinted down the left and, realising that Di Matteo was best left to shoot himself, declined to call for the ball. Di Matteo ran on for about forty yards before steadying himself for a right-foot shot. It was a nightmare scenario for Boro's England Under-21 goalkeeper Ben Roberts, who was only there because of injuries to two senior keepers. He faced the

prospect of conceding a goal before he had had a chance to make any kind of mark, even on the pitch as a 'sighter'.

It was a wickedly dipping shot which came down off the underside of the crossbar and behind the line. Trevor Brooking thought Roberts, six foot one and the son of a newsagent, might have done better to stop it. But the Norwich manager Mike

Walker, one of the few managers in this country to have been a goalkeeper, said: 'He had no chance. He had to come off his line to start with, otherwise he would have been criticised for staying on his line if Di Matteo shot either side of him.'

Perhaps if Roberts had been the same height as Billy Foulkes, Chelsea's legendary 20-stone goalkeeper, he might have tipped

Robbie Mustoe

Dennis Wise

Roberto Di Matteo

it over the bar. Foulkes was six foot five. No-one, or hardly anyone, noticed that Di Matteo was the only player on the field with his socks pulled up over his knees. 'I was very confused,' he said modestly. 'I just thought I would shoot and I was very lucky.'

John Motson, commentating in his last live Cup Final (unless the BBC win back the contract, which seems unlikely) won a lot of praise for saying almost immediately: 'That's 43 seconds, and if I'm not wrong, that's the fastest ever goal in a Final at Wembley. The previous record was held by Jackie Milburn who scored for Newcastle in 45 seconds in 1955.' Later, he mentioned that John Devey might have scored in 30 seconds for Aston Villa against West Bromwich Albion in 1895. He could be forgiven a minor blemish. The actual goalscorer was Bob Chatt and he scored in 40 seconds.

For the purpose of making it a competitive match, Boro, not

ROBERTO'S INSPIRATIONAL SISTER CONCETTA

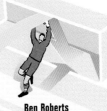

One of the proudest supporters at Wembley was Concetta Di Matteo, the sister of Roberto. When she was twelve, she contacted a rare eye disease, retinis pigmentosa, and by the time she was eighteen, all she could see was shadows. A relative sat next to her, talking her through the game.

'The way she has handled her problems had been an inspiration to me,' said Roberto. 'Hopefully, my success in England will now help her. She comes to London occasionally to stay with me. We are very close.'

Chelsea, should have scored first. The pace slowed and someone made the point that if all the players had been British that would not have happened. They would have played on at a frenetic pace. Only nine Englishmen were in the starting line-ups. The Continental influence had taken over.

Ben Roberts

Gianluca Festa

Mark Hughes

Roberto Di Matteo

Roberto Di Matteo

Dan Petrescu

TOP LEFT: This charming picture, taken at the Chelsea training ground, shows brother and sister Roberto and Concetta Di Matteo. The two are very close. Roberto dedicated his Cup Final goal to her.

OVERLEAF: You little beauty! Team-mates (right to left) Dennis Wise, Frank Sinclair, Scott Minto and Eddie Newton race to congratulate Roberto after his spectacular first-minute strike at Wembley.

Zola, who, like Juninho, looked tense, took a long time to show any of his skills. Near half-time he tested Roberts with a thirty-yard free-kick which curled round the right of the wall. The Boro keeper just managed to reach it. The kick was awarded by referee Steve Lodge – who had a commendable game – as Frank Leboeuf tumbled after a challenge by Craig Hignett. The young midfielder was clearly upset by Leboeuf's actions. 'You French b******,' he appeared to say.

In the few minutes before half-time, Chelsea's play was sloppy and Gullit rose to shout some advice, which no-one on the field could hear. The one moment of anxiety in the half came when Festa rose magnificently at the far post to head a cross from Phil Stamp past Frode Grodas. Countless replays on TV showed that the linesman was right when he flagged for offside. Yet so many mistakes are made by linesmen in these situations that it had to count as a slice of luck, especially as the flag didn't go up as Stamp connected, only a split-second later.

Gullit had his adviser, the Dutchman Ted Troost, sitting on the bench behind him. Troost is a practitioner in haptomie, which combines meditation with psychology. 'I asked him to speak to the players for the semi-final,' said Gullit. 'The reaction from the group, working on communication and dealing with stress, was good.' Troost worked with Gullit and his Dutch team-mate Marco van Basten in the 1988 European Championships. Van Basten, now retired, said at the time: 'We were like Formula One cars and Ted was our mechanic.'

In Holland, sports psychology is now an important part of the training of all coaches and it is incorporated in the coaching diploma, without which no coach can manage a top club. Most leading European soccer nations

LEFT: A typically determined Frank Leboeuf takes the ball away from Boro's Craig Hignett.

CENTRE: Zola starts to make an impression, as he evades this despairing lunge.

FAR LEFT: The battle between Mark Hughes and Gianluca Festa sees the Italian taking a ballet-style leap.

make it mandatory to have the top qualifications and there was pressure on the FA to follow their example. But when their new technical director Howard Wilkinson presented his 'Charter for Quality' the week after the Cup Final, there was no mention of mandatory qualifications being required in future for Premiership managers and coaches, half of whom are unqualified. Maybe a factor in that decision was the fact that Glenn Hoddle, the England coach, lacked the necessary qualifications. English football still believes that playing experience at the highest level is the best preparation for

management. Gullit, unqualified himself, which would debar him from coaching in Holland, was in the process of proving that can be right. His opposite number Bryan Robson was, however, casting doubts on the idea.

In the second half, the battle continued low key. It needed a run by Zola or Juninho to provide the detonator or even a few fifty-yard passes to stretch defenders. After almost an hour, Juninho at last broke clear and Di Matteo chopped him down just outside the area to concede a free-kick. As there were other defenders around, Mr Lodge showed Di

Matteo the yellow card not the red, a correct decision. Juninho's free-kick was harmless.

Four minutes later it was Zola's turn to be upended, by Festa. Mr Lodge rushed up, searching in his pocket for a card. Zola, sportingly,

Seventy-one minutes went by before Zola produced his first serious contribution.

tried to talk him out of it. Up went Lodge's arm, brandishing the yellow. Seventy-one minutes went by before Zola produced his first serious contribution, a mazy little dribble into the box which ended up with a shot from the right straight at Roberts.

Still the prospect remained that Boro might equalise and force extra-time. Bryan Robson's team had been taken to extra-time themselves against Leicester, in the Coca-Cola Cup final and replay, and Chesterfield, in the FA Cup semi-final at Old Trafford, and this was now the sixteenth Cup game of their season. Their players were mentally and physically drained, but still they ran and competed. That ought to be remembered when final assessments are made.

Boro had also played four Premiership matches in eight days in the final run-in, although for this they received less sympathy because one of those four fixtures was the controversially postponed game at Blackburn for which they had had points deducted. The decision to turn down their appeal had met with widespread approval, and only those on Teesside thought an injustice had been perpetrated.

Another factor in the general tiredness of the players at Wembley on May 17 was the unusually high humidity level. All round the country that day, swing bowlers were bowling sides out cheaply in the Britannic Assurance County Championship and next day the Australian tourists were dismissed for 121 at Worcester. 'It was not easy to keep running in those conditions,' said Gullit. The Wembley authorities do not allow players to be given those blue-coloured Lucozade bottles to top up during matches.

Mr Lodge was in action again when he cautioned Leboeuf for a foul on Juninho. From a quick free-kick taken by the Brazilian in the 80th minute, Vickers suddenly found himself bearing in on Norwegian goalkeeper Grodas. There was inattention in the Chelsea ranks. No-one went with him. Grodas had maintained his concentration level well and was perfectly positioned to make a blocking save with his legs. What if Vickers had pulled the ball back to a colleague, as well as he might?

English players are usually encouraged to shoot for the near post in these positions, or drive the ball along the six-yard box, hoping for a deflection. The Continentals, particularly the Italians, have shown us the value of the ball pulled back to the edge of the penalty area to oncoming players. Afterwards Gullit said: 'They did not have one shot on target.' He was wrong. They had one, the Vickers effort.

LEFT: Eyes on the prize . . . and the ball. Juninho's free-kick is blocked by the Chelsea wall of **(left to right) Hughes, Minto, Clarke, Newton and Di Matteo as Boro press for the equaliser.**

ABOVE: Eddie Newton knocks in the second goal off Nigel Pearson's arm and turns away

(ABOVE RIGHT) as Mark Hughes celebrates and Boro's keeper Ben Roberts dives in vain.

It was entirely fitting that the second and decisive goal should be scored by Eddie Newton. When he played in the 1994 FA Cup Final, with the score at 0-0 he gave away a penalty against Manchester United and Chelsea went on to lose 4-0. He described it as the worst moment of his life. Then he was out for eight months with a broken leg and he underwent a knee operation just after Christmas, 1996. 'It's been a slog getting back, but this has made it all worthwhile,' he said. The move that led to the goal was started by a perceptive cross from the right, wide of the far post, and Zola, realising he was too close to the byeline to shoot, performed a ballet-style flick with his right leg to divert the ball back across goal. Newton and Hughes were rushing up and it was Newton who was closest, and his shot went in off Pearson's right hand.

Graham Rix signalled to Vialli to warm up and to cheers from the Chelsea ranks, the Italian did several energetic runs up the track. Vialli had pleaded the day before: 'Please give me five minutes.' Gullit was to give him two. Zola, the man Vialli replaced, was delighted, bowing to him as he walked off and smiling broadly. There was time for Vialli to touch the ball once before Mr Lodge blew his Acme Tornado 2000 pealess whistle for the final time. The joy of the players was matched by the joy of the Chelsea supporters. They hugged and kissed each other. Gullit joined in and was so overcome with the emotion of it all that he had to be reminded by FA administration officer Adrian Titcombe that he too was entitled to receive a medal from the Duchess of Kent.

The after-match celebrations went on for a long time, much longer than usual, and a highlight was the lining-up of the players, some wearing wigs and Grodas a Viking helmet, for a race down the pitch. Wise was the man carrying the Cup and when he reached the penalty area he threw himself to the ground, making sure that when he landed the Cup was cradled in his chest.

Gullit gestured to Ken Bates, who had remained in the emptying Royal Box, to join them and eventually he did, almost tripping over as he walked down the steps past the grasping hands of his worshippers.

THE FACTS ABOUT A 'HALF-DECENT' FINAL

CHELSEA		MIDDLESBROUGH
2	Goals	0
6	Attempts on target	1
1	Attempts off target	4
12	Free-kicks	14
8	Corners	3
5	Offsides	16
3	Bookings	1
0	Sendings-off	0

Bates had embraced most of his players when they collected their medals and now he was to do it again. Zola danced a jig, and as he left the pitch he poured a big bottle of water over his head. The Chelsea interviews in the press room next to the St John's Ambulance room had to be delayed, so long did the delirium go on. The Boro contingent were quickly in and out.

'We didn't perform, we were well beaten,' said Bryan Robson. 'Still, I'd rather be beaten in the Final than the first round. It's bad enough being beaten in a Cup Final but to lose two and be relegated hurts so much. Now I've got a lot of work to do this summer and make decisions which will get us back in the Premier League.'

Juninho was dignified in defeat. 'It has been very bad to lose so many things in one season,' he said. 'Now I must do what is best for me and my career. I want to play in the World Cup Final next year for Brazil and I don't think it will be good for my international career to be playing in the Nationwide First Division.'

For Ravanelli it was a similar story. He looked totally dejected from the moment he limped off, and he admitted afterwards: 'I was not 100 per cent. My left leg was not sustaining my right one, but I felt I had to play as a sign of respect to the fans and the team. It was a great occasion but luck was not with me. I felt the injury as soon as I pushed for the ball and I couldn't carry on.'

Zola and Di Matteo represented the upside of buying foreign stars. Ravanelli, Vialli, Emerson and maybe even Juninho represented the downside. Although Juninho had had a remarkable season, his club had failed in two Cup finals and been relegated. It was nothing to put on his CV.

Festa, too, wanted to join the Riverside exodus. 'I cannot swallow so many bad things,' he said expressively. 'I'm going back home and I will be leaving my mobile phone switched-on.'

RIGHT: The two goalscorers congratulate each other at the final whistle. Di Matteo (right) still has his socks pulled up over his knees!

BOTTOM LEFT: Ruud Gullit leads the celebrations on the bench after Eddie Newton's goal. Graham Rix (extreme right) can hardly contain himself!

OVERLEAF: The moment every Chelsea fan had been waiting for, as Dennis Wise lifts the trophy.

The last word on Di Matteo came from Graham Rix, the man who puffs away on his Clint Eastwood-style cheroots as he surveys what is going on around him. 'You look at Robbie and you think there are better tacklers, better passers and better goalscorers, but then you see who has come out on top against him and you are struggling to count them on the fingers of one hand,' he said.

'He, more than any other player in our side, runs games. He sets the tempo with his ability to quicken or slow the game down. His passing is deadly accurate and there is nobody in the country better at finishing from midfield, including David Beckham.'

More than an hour after the finish, Gullit was still giving interviews. 'I knew there was more to this team than they showed last year,' he said. 'But when you haven't won anything, you do not know what it is like to achieve it. Now they do and they will be better for it. They did not know what their limits were. Now they realise they can win trophies.

'I am a bit more proud to win as a manager than as a player. I had a hand in everything we did and it meant I could shape the team as I wanted it. I was lucky in a way that I was injured, because that gave me more time to concentrate on the team. I might have been able to play, I don't know. But it was best if I didn't.

'I have matured as a person. I demand 100 per cent from myself and give people around me responsibility, which is important. I don't want to be afraid to make decisions. We all make mistakes, but it is good because you learn from them. I was honest with everyone and gave everyone the same chances. When I started, some players weren't so happy and wanted to leave. Fine, that was alright by me. Those that stayed now know what I want from this club and how we can achieve it.'

Much was written in the days before the Final about whether Gullit would be signing a new contract. It was not really an issue. He still had a year on his existing contract and he said:

'I am happy to stay. I am not thinking about leaving. The contract is something between me and Ken Bates. Ken deserves this. He has worked hard for it. We should also remember Matthew Harding and what he did for the club. He has been with us in spirit all the season.' Ruth Harding, Matthew's widow, watched the

'I knew there was more to this team than they showed last year. Now they realise they can win trophies.'

game from the Royal Box in her capacity as patron of the club. 'I will do all I can to see that we continue supporting the club,' she said.

The Wembley staff had to clear up in preparation for the FA Trophy final between Dagenham & Redbridge and Woking the next day. It was time to go.

LEFT: An ecstatic chairman (far left) leads the Royal Box in applauding his players.

BELOW: The prolonged celebrations on the pitch provided some of the best pictures in FA Cup history.

DENNIS WISE'S MAGIC SLIPPERS

Every FA Cup Final side needs a gimmick. In 1983, the Brighton manager Jimmy Melia gloried in the publicity over his lucky white dancing-shoes. But after the Seagulls had held Manchester United to a 2-2 draw in the first match, Melia's luck ran out as United won the replay 4-0.

Chelsea were short of one until Dennis Wise suddenly disclosed on the eve of the Final that he had a special pair of slippers. They were a Christmas present. He said, 'If you press them, they play a tune. They play "Whatever will be, will be, We're going to Wembley." I press them every time before a Cup game.'

Some of the foreign players wanted extra tickets for the banquet at the Waldorf Hotel in the Aldwych, and they had to be disappointed because there were not enough to go round. The club was loyal to those members of staff who had helped so much over the years. By 3am the first of them were making their way home. The players stayed overnight.

The FA Cup was in the charge of Gwyn Williams, who insisted on having it next to his bed as he slept. The previous time Chelsea had won it, the chairman Brian Mears actually insisted that his wife June should vacate their double bed so he could sleep with the Cup. Mears was present at the 1997 Final. 'I loved every minute,' he said.

Next morning, the players' sponsored sunglasses came out to disguise hangovers. The ceremonial parade took them to Fulham Town Hall for a reception and more speeches. Bates was given a presidential-style welcome as he later walked down the King's Road, only to be taken aback when a man threw a pint of beer over him. 'I was so annoyed, I gave chase,' he told the *Daily Mirror*, whose football reporter Harry Harris lives a short distance from Stamford Bridge. 'Just imagine it. I am 65 and he was about 28, but after giving him a

four-yard start I caught up with him in twenty. Admittedly he was about eighteen stone, a big fat bar steward, you might say.

'I swung him round and was about to land one on him when about five Chelsea supporters grabbed me from behind and stopped me. They said, "You don't need this, just carry on shaking

hands and having a good time." They grabbed the bloke and the last I saw of him, he was receiving a well-placed boot up the backside. Mind you, it was very hot and having beer over me only served to refresh me. He looked like a man who regretted starting on me in the first place. I admit I had a few. But I think I

ought to get into the *Guinness Book of Records* for that chase.'

Later in the afternoon, the players boarded the coach again for the trip to Heathrow to fly to Hong Kong for the first of their end-of-season matches. The laughing and the joking were over by then. It was time to catch up on some sleep.

One of Ruud Gullit's few embarrassing moments of the campaign came when he was told that the players would like a 'perks pool' before the FA Cup Final. This is the English footballer's traditional way of earning himself some extra cash from personal appearances, advertising, and giving interviews.

On the Continent, these promotional activities are part of the job of being a footballer. No payments are offered, and none demanded.

When Chelsea reached the 1994 FA Cup Final the players entrusted their affairs to Eric Hall, an agent who has considerable experience, some might say notoriety, in these matters. It caused a lot of resentment, especially from the newspaper correspondents who did not like being told whom they could interview and for how much. Of course, this tradition would have long since died out if the newspapers, radio stations and TV companies had refused to pay for something that should

FAR LEFT: The goalscorers hold the Cup aloft.

ABOVE AND OVERLEAF: It's West London's turn to celebrate, the following day.

The ceremonial double-decker bus threads its way through the throng in the Fulham Road. 'It was like VE-Day,' said one Chelsea pensioner.

have been theirs by right. Some newspapers were still trying to outdo each other by buying up certain players and making their uninteresting remarks 'exclusive'. The rise in newsprint costs, plus the increase in other costs, were now forcing sports editors to reduce expenditure. More and more newspapers refused to pay.

Gullit had had to field a tricky question at his first press conference following the semi-final win over Wimbledon. 'With so many players earning fortunes, are these demeaning activities really necessary?' one reporter asked him. Gullit looked uneasy. 'It is something we cannot avoid,' he said. 'But it is new to me and it is a distraction.'

Someone asked how the money would be shared out. If a player was earning £10,000 a week, did he really need to rush around performing these functions to bring in a further £5-10,000 a man, depending on how successful the pool turned out to be? 'Maybe you should ask the players,' replied Gullit. 'I think some of the money will go to charity. Some will go to the cooks and the background staff. Everyone is involved. It is not just the players.' Someone interjected that in 1994 a donation had been made to the Great Ormond Street Hospital. The same thing would happen this time. It all had an unsavoury ring about it and Gullit's distaste was evident. English footballers are years behind their Continental equivalents in knowing how to project themselves in public, how to conduct an interview. It is one of the reasons why Gianfranco Zola has proved so popular. He knows how to talk to the press – for nothing.

Later, stories emerged in some newspapers about how much money the agent Paul Stretford, appointed by the players to handle the pool, was charging for interviews. The best-known players like Zola, Vialli and Mark Hughes would command a fee of £12,000. Ordinary players like Frank Sinclair and Eddie Newton would need a fee of £6,000, those on the fringe a mere £2,000. Zola, significantly, still did an interview for the *Mail on Sunday* which bore the tailpiece: 'No money was paid for this interview.'

There was some bad publicity for the club when it was revealed that the Chelsea players had not been made available for interview for the official FA Cup Final programme. Stretford explained that there had been a mix-up. The players were not asking for money to appear in the programme. But the programme went to press without quotes from Gullit's players.

No FA Cup Final is played without a ticket controversy being uncovered, and this time it was the revelation in the *News of the World* that Ken Bates was selling tickets as part of a corporate hospitality package costing almost £600. An FA official said sternly that no club was allowed to sell FA Cup Final tickets in such a manner. But as the FA were doing the same thing themselves, for a similar price, they were not in a strong position to take any action. Bates reminded them of that fact.

A Chelsea member told David Mellor on the *Six-O-Six* radio programme that he and his wife and four daughters, all regulars at Stamford Bridge, had not been able to obtain tickets, although they had fulfilled all the criteria. The caller claimed that only 20,000 tickets had gone to members. Where had the other 5,000 gone? Mellor promised to take the matter up with the Chelsea chairman. It was just one of many complaints. However well-organised the distribution, the innocent and most loyal are often the ones to suffer.

Meanwhile, the Chelsea song had been recorded. Gullit, predictably, did not take part. 'Maybe it should have been an Italian song,' joked Vialli.

ABOVE LEFT: Zola dons a wig as he poses for yet another happy snap – but his medal has pride of place in his right hand.

RIGHT: It's the turn of the player-manager to pose with the trophy. This was one of the proudest moments of Gullit's career.

On the Monday before the Cup Final, a fax arrived at media offices saying that Chelsea had changed their plans about interviews and there would be daily press conferences with assigned players and no fee would be charged. It was a complete climbdown. Steve Clarke, the longest-serving player, willingly undertook the role of spokesman. At 33, the highly-respected Scot proved an ideal choice.

'We are very upset about the negative publicity this issue has attracted,' he said. 'The proceeds from the pool will be distributed among all the staff, from the ladies who clean the kit and run the canteen to the YTS boys.

'If we didn't have a pool, the big-name players could take the money for themselves by doing exclusives. This way, everyone gets a share. We're giving 10 per cent to the Great Ormond Street Hospital – and that decision was made before we got all this bad press.'

Standing nearby was Paul Stretford who, like most agents,

PREVIOUS PAGE: Frank Leboeuf (left) and Gianluca Vialli lead the players' own particular tribute to the Chelsea boss.

RIGHT: Pure joy is registered on the face of Steve Clarke, a great Chelsea servant, as he clutches his medal and the trophy.

charges a sizeable commission. He was destined to be one of the largest beneficiaries.

Clarke, whose testimonial year it was, made a pertinent point about the progress of the club. 'I've been here since the bad old days,' he said. 'We stuttered from season to season with no real purpose.

'Glenn Hoddle arrived here three years ago and changed all that. We got to the FA Cup Final in his first year, and things have improved every year and we now have the best squad I have ever seen here.'

Around this time Chelsea could have fielded an entire team of foreigners and Clarke made another sound point. 'It would be good to see a couple of British players signed to keep the balance right,' he said. 'You need players who know what the Premiership is all about. I feel

FLOWERS FOR LEICESTER

On April 18, the day before the home Premiership match against Leicester, Ruud Gullit made an unusual request to Gwyn Williams (pictured left). 'I want you to order twenty bouquets of flowers to present to the Leicester squad,' he said. Williams was mystified. He knew that Leicester had just won the Coca-Cola Cup, beating Middlesbrough in the replayed final – but flowers?

'We don't do that sort of thing here,' he said. 'It's not part of our tradition.' But Gullit explained that it was commonplace in European football to present flowers to a team after they had won a big event. 'You see,' he said. 'It will be a nice touch and they will like it.'

Williams rang Leicester to put the idea to them and one of their officials expressed no opposition. So when the Leicester players came out of the tunnel at Stamford Bridge the next day, they were confronted by the Chelsea players lined-up in a guard of honour, bouquets in their hands.

The presentation went off well, the crowd clapped and cheered and the Leicester players showed no sign of embarrassment.

the foreign boys will be the first to admit that some of the games here have been a culture shock.'

In the new culture of big-name players moving from club to club, country to country, usually at the instigation at their agent, one was left to wonder whether there would be another Steve Clarke-type loyalist in ten years' time, qualifying for a testimonial. Somehow, it had to be doubted.

Clarke was right about Hoddle's reforming zeal. Gwyn Williams

confirmed: 'When Glenn came, he changed everything. He wanted everything done his way and he didn't miss a thing. For example, he insisted that there should be

'I've been here since the bad old days... and we now have the best squad I have ever seen here.'

facilities to water the main pitch at the training ground so it would be just like the surface at Stamford Bridge.'

Hoddle had been the architect, Gullit the master builder.

EN ROUTE TO WEMBLEY 1997

THIRD ROUND

Saturday 4 January
Chelsea 3   West Brom 0

A predictably easy victory over struggling Nationwide First Division opposition. Dennis Wise opened the scoring in the first half, Craig Burley got the second after coming on as a substitute, and Gianfranco Zola settled it by adding the third on his FA Cup debut.

FOURTH ROUND

Sunday 26 January
Chelsea 4   Liverpool 2

It was after this game that the thought emerged that maybe this was Chelsea's year for the Cup. In a one-sided first half Fowler and Collymore gave Liverpool a 2-0 lead, but Ruud Gullit sent on Mark Hughes for the second half and the game changed as he recorded Chelsea's first. Zola had the crowd roaring with a fantastic equaliser, and two goals from Gianluca Vialli completed an amazing transformation.

FIFTH ROUND

Sunday 16 February
Leicester 2   Chelsea 2

Goals from Roberto Di Matteo and Mark Hughes put Chelsea 2-0 ahead at half-time but the contest turned around later. Poor defending against high crosses led to Steve Walsh heading in Leicester's first, and near the end Eddie Newton turned the ball into his own goal to give the home side a replay. Ruud Gullit upset his opposite number Martin O'Neill by claiming the home side were lucky.

FIFTH ROUND REPLAY
Wednesday 26 February
Chelsea 1   Leicester 0   (aet)

The most controversial moment of the season. Leicester were hanging on three minutes from the end of extra-time when Erland Johnsen crashed into Spencer Prior just inside the penalty area and referee Mike Reed was about the only person present who thought it was a penalty. Frank Leboeuf calmly converted. O'Neill and his players were furious.

SIXTH ROUND
Sunday 9 March
Portsmouth 1   Chelsea 4

Pompey's youngsters froze as chairman Terry Venables and manager Terry Fenwick erred by playing three at the back against world-class forwards. It was all over once Mark Hughes volleyed a brilliant first. Dennis Wise added two more before Zola scored the fourth. Substitute Deon Burton replied for the outclassed home side.

SEMI-FINAL
Sunday 13 April (at Highbury)
Chelsea 3   Wimbledon 0

Another seemingly difficult task completed with plenty to spare. A nervous Dons side realised it was over once Mark Hughes scored just before the interval, and when Zola netted a brilliant second the celebrations began. Hughes scored the third near the end. Semi finals are rarely classics. This one was almost an anti-climax.

LEFT: A Mark Hughes goal sparks the great comeback after he had come on as a half-time substitute against Liverpool.

RIGHT: Gianfranco Zola celebrates after his stunning piece of individual skill puts Chelsea 2-0 up in the semi-final against Wimbledon.

PAST TRIUMPHS

Former England manager Ron Greenwood, who appeared in half the matches that season for Chelsea, recalled: 'It was totally different in those days. Today, it's all about money. Everything seems out of proportion and I can't make any sense of it. Money never came into it with us. It was nitty-gritty stuff.'

Greenwood was a commanding, intelligent centre-half whose career as a coach was already well underway when he was at Stamford Bridge. He also remembered that 'there was no social scene at the club. The players turned up, trained or played, and that was it.'

It was vastly different when Chelsea's next success came along, the winning of the FA Cup in 1970. A number of players then were renowned for their drinking exploits. One, Tommy Baldwin, was even known as 'The Sponge' because of his ability to soak it up. They were befriended by pop singers, film stars and starlets, anyone whose name frequently appeared in the gossip columns.

Twenty-six years on, the trend has swung back towards the puritanism of the Fifties, with the players actively discouraged from excessive anything - drinking, eating or partying. This new culture, imported from Europe, has made the players fitter and sharper. But are they better?

ABOVE: Ted Drake, Chelsea's manager when they won the title in 1954-55. One of the game's gentlemen, he died, aged 82, in May 1995.

FAR RIGHT: Ron Greenwood in action in 1955. A studious player with a deep knowledge of tactics, he went on to manage England.

The first time Chelsea lifted a major trophy was in the 1954-55 season when they won the First Division title with 52 points, the lowest winning total since 1914-15. It was, most people outside of west London agreed, an undistinguished year.

Just as it is impossible to compare the boxing champions of one age with those of another, so it is impossible to assess which set of players would come out on top. As Sir Stanley Matthews once told me: 'In our day the balls were heavier and harder to pass, on pitches that were not as good as today's. The food wasn't as good. The referees let the players get on with it, not like it is today. And there was much more tackling.'

In the winter of 1954-55, the air was not as clean either. The Clean Air Act was still a year off and often a heavy fog shrouded Stamford Bridge. There were fifty professionals on the staff, none earning more than £16-20 a week, when Ted Drake, the former Arsenal centre-forward and Hampshire cricketer, took over as manager in 1952.

Drake signed Greenwood from Brentford for £16,000 – a weekly wage for a star player these days – and for less, John McNichol, the Brighton inside-forward, who could be likened to Gianfranco Zola. In his autobiography, *Yours Sincerely*, Greenwood said of McNichol: 'He was the first player I saw really curve shots and passes with the outside of his foot. He was a player who made things happen and was famous for his "Bovril" ball, as we called it, a long pass hit towards a Bovril advertisement in one of the

corners. Eric Parsons, fleet of foot on the wing, always used to chase it. We called him "Rabbit" because he showed the soles of his boots as he ran.'

Chelsea were champions because they played to their strengths and, despite indifferent home form,

were more consistent that season than the average Chelsea side. Greenwood also felt the players had a greater affinity with the supporters in those days than they do today, 'because the players used to travel to the ground by train and got to know them.'

	P	W	D	L	F	A	Pts
Chelsea	42	20	12	10	81	57	52
Wolverhampton W	42	19	10	13	89	70	48
Portsmouth	42	18	12	12	74	62	48
Sunderland	42	15	18	9	64	54	48
Manchester U	42	20	7	15	84	74	47
Aston Villa	42	20	7	15	72	73	47
Manchester C	42	18	10	14	76	69	46
Newcastle U	42	17	9	16	89	77	43
Arsenal	42	17	9	16	69	63	43
Burnley	42	17	9	16	51	48	43
Everton	42	16	10	16	62	68	42
Huddersfield	42	14	13	15	63	68	41
Sheffield U	42	17	7	18	70	86	41
Preston N E	42	16	8	18	83	64	40
Charlton Ath	42	15	10	17	76	75	40
Tottenham H	42	16	8	18	72	73	40
WBA	42	16	8	18	76	96	40
Bolton W	42	13	13	16	62	69	39
Blackpool	42	14	10	18	60	64	38
Cardiff C	42	13	11	18	62	76	37
Leicester C	42	12	11	19	74	86	35
Sheffield W	42	8	10	24	63	100	26

TITLE TRIVIA

Chelsea lost as many matches at home as they did away. At one point they went six home matches without a win, losing four. They gained only 27 points at home, achieving 25 on their travels.

The Blues achieved 'the double' over runners-up Wolves but were beaten home and away by Manchester United.

As champions, Chelsea should have been England's first entrants in the new European Cup the following season, but the authorities advised them to withdraw because of possible fixture congestion.

Their FA Cup campaign was less successful. After defeating Walsall (D3S) and Bristol Rovers (D2), Chelsea lost 1-0 in the fifth round at Second Division Notts County.

The late Roy Bentley was the Peter Osgood of the side, a centre-forward with a delicate touch and good skills both in the air and on the ground. Bentley and most of his colleagues had served in the War or, like the young left-winger Frank Blunstone, were doing their National Service. They were naturally fit, and as the writer John Moynihan observed: 'There was something almost military about the Chelsea team, boots highly-polished, hair well-combed, shoulders back, chests out - the boys got down to work with a zest.'

Bill Robertson was the first-choice goalkeeper until he was injured and Chick Thomson took over. The full-backs were tough, resourceful characters: Peter Sillett (brother of John), who blasted in the penalties, and the much-feared Stan Willemse, with the experienced John Harris in reserve. The half-back line, as it was known in those days, was Ken Armstrong, who played for England before emigrating to New Zealand; Greenwood, until he was replaced by Steve Wicks from Reading; and the former amateur from Walthamstow Avenue, Derek Saunders. The inside-forwards, or attacking midfield players, were McNichol and Les Stubbs, with Parsons and Blunstone on the wings. Bentley was to end the season with 21 goals.

Ask any older Chelsea supporter which was the most exciting match ever played at Stamford Bridge and he might well opt for the Chelsea v Manchester United First Division match on October 16, 1954. It was the debut game of Seamus O'Connell, an amateur signed from Bishop Auckland, and he scored a hat-trick only to finish on the losing side. Chelsea were 5-2 down at one stage before losing 6-5. Eight goals came in a frantic period of thirty minutes.

Greenwood tells a story of the goal headed in by Tommy Taylor, the England centre-forward from Barnsley who was to lose his life in the Munich air disaster four years later. Taylor got up so well to power the ball into the net that Greenwood said to him as he fell: 'What a great goal!' The normally mild-mannered Drake was upset when the players returned to the dressing-room at half-time.

'What are you doing?' he asked Greenwood. 'Stand on his toes so he can't get off the ground next time!' Greenwood moved on to Fulham as Chelsea started rising up the table in the second half of the season. His replacement Wicks won his place in the side on merit.

The game Chelsea needed to win was against Wolves – the leading club side in the country following their floodlit friendly successes over Spartak of Russia and Honved of Hungary – and it was

LEFT: The late Roy Bentley. An England international, he scored some remarkable goals in Chelsea's title-winning season.

played in front of 75,000 fans on Easter Saturday. The Wolves forward-line boasted England wingers Johnny Hancocks and Jimmy Mullen, and also in the side were Bert Williams, Ron Flowers and the legendary Billy Wright. The match was heading for a draw when O'Connell sent a long-range shot past Williams only for Wright to punch it away. The referee awarded a corner. Chelsea's players complained, though not as volubly as today's players would have done in similar circumstances. The fans,

however, roared their disapproval and after a few seconds, the official went to consult his linesman. After some agonising deliberation, the referee pointed towards the penalty spot. 'It was

The game Chelsea needed to win was against Wolves and it was played in front of 75,000 fans on Easter Saturday.

Peter's most terrifying moment of his career,' said John Sillett. 'Bert Williams was standing there like a ruddy elephant. Peter gave it everything he'd got and it went in like a steam engine out of control.'

Tony Banks, who was appointed Sports Minister when the Tony Blair administration took over just before the 1997 FA Cup Final, was an 11-year-old in the crowd that day, barely able to see what was going on. 'Peter was an incredibly powerful kicker of a dead ball,' Banks recalled. 'It didn't seem to rise more than a few inches above the ground into the bottom left-hand corner of the net, right in front of where I was standing.

'I'd been going with my Dad for two or three years and I've got all my programmes from that season, and I still re-read them. My great hero was Roy Bentley, who also played for England. There was Eric Parsons, Stan Williams, Frank Blunstone, the late Ken Armstrong and Stan Wicks, a great centre-half, and Bill Robertson the goalkeeper. I see Eric and Stan Wicks fairly regularly and as far as I'm concerned, they're still

RIGHT: Left-winger Frank Blunstone was doing his National Service in 1954-55 but always found time to play.

BELOW: Eric Parsons, who played on the other wing, was renowned as the fastest player in the side.

great heroes. I am far more overawed in their company than I am with politicians, film stars or modern-day sports people.' Banks used to travel to matches from his home in Brixton on the number

45 bus. Making the same journey, though they did not know each other at the time, was the future Prime Minister John Major.

Chelsea had to beat Sheffield Wednesday at the Bridge to make sure of the title, and though they won 3-0 they had to wait fifteen minutes after the finish before it was confirmed that Portsmouth had drawn 1-1 at Cardiff and could not catch them. Joe Mears, the chairman, made a short speech and called on Drake, whose Hampshire burr seemed out of place, to follow him.

'At the start of the season I was asked if I thought we might win the Cup,' said Drake. 'I thought we might, but I thought we had a

greater chance of winning the title. I congratulate all the boys and every one of my staff, office, training and playing. Right throughout, they are one and all Chelsea.' Drake always called the players 'my boys', even the ones in their thirties. He was a man of great warmth and compassion, almost too nice, some said, to be a football manager.

Brian Mears, who was to succeed his father as chairman, said: 'It was a fantastic moment and the nice thing about it was that it was the club's 50th anniversary year. What a way to celebrate! Not only that, but we also won all the other prizes that season, the Football Combination, the Met League and the South East Counties League.'

It was an elderly team and Drake had already started drafting in teenagers. The greatest striker in the club's history, Jimmy Greaves, was among them. Soon after the 6-5 epic against Manchester United, Drake had received a telephone call from his chief scout, Jimmy Thompson.

'I've just seen the most exciting game I've ever seen,' said Drake.

'Don't worry about that,' replied Thompson. 'I've just seen the best player I've ever seen.' Thompson tended to say that about a lot of players, but when he saw Greaves in action Drake knew that this time he was right.

CHELSEA'S LEAGUE FIXTURES 1954-55

Aug 21	LEICESTER CITY (A)	Drew	1-1
Aug 23	BURNLEY (H)	Won	1-0
Aug 28	BOLTON WANDERERS (H)	Won	3-2
Aug 31	BURNLEY (A)	Drew	1-1
Sep 4	CARDIFF CITY (H)	Drew	1-1
Sep 6	PRESTON NORTH END (H)	Lost	0-1
Sep 11	MANCHESTER CITY (A)	Drew	1-1
Sep 15	PRESTON NORTH END (A)	Won	2-1
Sep 18	EVERTON (H)	Lost	0-2
Sep 20	SHEFFIELD UNITED (A)	Won	2-1
Sep 25	NEWCASTLE UNITED (A)	Won	3-1
Oct 2	WEST BROMWICH ALBION (H)	Drew	3-3
Oct 9	HUDDERSFIELD TOWN (A)	Lost	0-1
Oct 16	MANCHESTER UNITED (H)	Lost	5-6
Oct 23	BLACKPOOL (A)	Won	1-0
Oct 30	CHARLTON ATHLETIC (H)	Lost	1-2
Nov 6	SUNDERLAND (A)	Drew	3-3
Nov 13	TOTTENHAM HOTSPUR (H)	Won	2-1
Nov 20	SHEFFIELD WEDNESDAY (A)	Drew	1-1
Nov 27	PORTSMOUTH (H)	Won	4-1
Dec 4	WOLVERHAMPTON WANDERERS (A)	Won	4-3
Dec 11	ASTON VILLA (H)	Won	4-0
Dec 18	LEICESTER CITY (H)	Won	3-1
Dec 25	ARSENAL (A)	Lost	0-1
Dec 27	ARSENAL (H)	Drew	1-1
Jan 1	BOLTON WANDERERS (A)	Lost	2-5
Jan 22	MANCHESTER CITY (H)	Lost	0-2
Feb 5	EVERTON (A)	Drew	1-1
Feb 12	NEWCASTLE UNITED (H)	Won	4-3
Feb 26	HUDDERSFIELD TOWN (H)	Won	4-1
Mar 5	ASTON VILLA (A)	Won	3-2
Mar 9	WEST BROMWICH ALBION (A)	Won	4-2
Mar 12	BLACKPOOL (H)	Drew	0-0
Mar 19	CHARLTON ATHLETIC (A)	Lost	0-2
Mar 23	CARDIFF CITY (A)	Won	1-0
Mar 29	SUNDERLAND (H)	Won	2-1
Apr 2	TOTTENHAM HOTSPUR (A)	Won	4-2
Apr 8	SHEFFIELD UNITED (H)	Drew	1-1
Apr 9	WOLVERHAMPTON WANDERERS (H)	Won	1-0
Apr 16	PORTSMOUTH (A)	Drew	0-0
Apr 23	SHEFFIELD WEDNESDAY (H)	Won	3-0
Apr 30	MANCHESTER UNITED (A)	Lost	1-2

Greaves lasted until 1961 when he was sold, unhappily and briefly, to AC Milan for £80,000. In four seasons for Chelsea he scored 124 goals in 157 League matches, including five against West Bromwich Albion and five against Wolves, which ended Billy Wright's career. I was present at that match. It was an extraordinary performance by an extraordinary talent.

The Drake reign was followed by the altogether different Docherty reign. Under the wise-cracking Tommy Doc, Stamford Bridge was a stimulating place to be on a Saturday afternoon. Volatile and inspirational, Docherty was totally unpredictable but he produced an exciting side although, like almost every other Chelsea side, one lacking in consistency. Promoted in 1962-63, they won the League Cup in 1965 and were runners-up in the FA Cup in 1967. The next season, Docherty was ousted.

When football clubs change their manager after a turbulent period, they usually go for an opposite, especially if the man being replaced is a Docherty. The new man was Dave Sexton, a calm, orderly student of the game with a decent, rational approach to everything and everyone.

Shy, almost retiring, he was much more interested in coaching and tactics than the razzmatazz of running the newsiest club in London. He kept the nucleus of Docherty's squad and added steadfast characters like the Cockney David Webb, bought from Southampton for £60,000; John Dempsey, who came from Fulham for the same amount; and Ian Hutchinson, signed from Cambridge United, who had a forty-yard throw.

One of Sexton's most interesting young players was the teenager from the prefab across the other side of the King's Road, Alan Hudson. Prefabs were cheap, hastily-constructed small houses built after World War II to solve the nation's housing crisis. With little space to sit around in, they were open invitations to youngsters to pop outside and kick footballs about on the remaining bomb-sites, or in the streets. That was where Hudson, one of the game's unfulfilled talents, learned his trade. With the right sort of encouragement and

A key factor in the quarter-final success was the way Ron Harris kept Rodney Marsh in check.

background he might well have gone on to become one of his country's greatest midfield players. As it was, he ended up with just two England caps despite a hugely promising debut. A tragic waste.

Chelsea's 1970 FA Cup campaign was typically

inconsistent though the same players, with the odd exception, appeared in every match. An easy 3-0 win over Birmingham in the third round was followed by a sticky 2-2 draw against Burnley at home in the fourth. The replay was won conclusively by 3-1 and a fifth-round trip to Crystal Palace proved just as rewarding, with a 4-1 victory. A key factor in the quarter-final success at QPR, 4-2, was the way the often under-valued Ron Harris kept Rodney Marsh in check. The semi-final against Second Division opponents turned out to be a rout, with Watford goalkeeper Mike Walker, now manager of Norwich, being beaten five times in a 5-1 mismatch. In the other semi-final, Leeds and Manchester United twice drew 0-0 in titanic matches before a rare goal from Billy Bremner saw Don Revie's controversial and unloved side through to Wembley. The quality of their football commanded more respect than their so-called 'professionalism', which nowadays many would consider cheating.

ABOVE LEFT: Dave Sexton ponders how he can improve things on the pitch. Behind Sexton is his assistant Tommy Cavanagh.

RIGHT: The indomitable Ron Harris, one of football's greatest tacklers and imtimidators, leads out the Chelsea team.

Most Chelsea supporters of that time will remember how Eddie Gray tormented David Webb in the first match at Wembley on April 11 which ended in a 2-2 draw. 'There had been so much warming up down the King's Road, I don't think some of the players were in the right frame of mind for it,' said Webb. 'Too many of us went to have a good day out rather than win. Leeds went there to win and were much the better side. But we hung on to get a second chance. We had resilience and that's a thing that counts.'

Peter Osgood, who scored eight goals in the Cup run, including a goal or more in every round, couldn't believe the state of the Wembley pitch when he went out to inspect it with his colleagues. 'They'd held a horse show on it some time before and the drains got broken,' he said. 'The greatest pitch in the world was more like a cabbage patch. I always think we would not have needed a replay if it had been in its usual state. On a good surface, we had the players to have won it first time.'

The first goal scored by Leeds was partly caused by the pitch. Jack Charlton headed an Eddie Gray cross towards Eddie McCreadie on the line and as McCreadie shaped to block the ball it refused to bounce and trickled under his foot and over the line. It was like a batsman

being bowled by a shooter in a Test match at Lord's. Then just before the interval, the late, much-lamented Peter Houseman essayed a shot at Gary Sprake who somehow managed to fumble the ball over the line. He was to be dropped for the replay, David Harvey taking over.

Seven minutes from full-time, Mick Jones hit a rebound past Peter Bonetti – Leeds had won something at last and deservedly so, it seemed. There was plenty of chit-chat between the players, and Osgood remembers an exchange he had with Norman Hunter. 'Ian Hutchinson always played with his socks rolled down and Norman caught him late,' he told the *Daily Mirror*'s Nigel Clarke, a lifelong Chelsea fan. "You wouldn't be in the team if it wasn't for your long throw," Norman said to him. Five minutes later Hutch headed the equaliser. "Ask him what he thinks now," I told him. I also told Norman I would score against him in the replay. He wouldn't have it. But I did and I'm the last player to have scored in every round.'

In those dreadful conditions, the players were unable to score again in the extra half-hour and it was up to Old Trafford eighteen days later for a replay, the first ever after a Cup Final at Wembley and the first since 1912. Geoffrey Green, the lyrical football writer of *The Times*, wrote of the second

chapter in the saga: 'It was no match for weaklings. Here was a match of gleaming steel, mostly with the broadsword which was used with impunity by both sides and allowed to be used by a referee who would have a short life in Latin America.'

Sexton made a tactical change in defence, switching Harris to right-back to stop Gray and moving Webb into the centre of defence to partner Dempsey. Harris carried out his instructions with

almost ruthless efficiency. In one of his early tackles, he left Gray writhing on the ground and the Scots winger was finished. Referee Eric Jennings was so indulgent by today's standards of refereeing, said Webb, that both sides would have finished up with eight men nowadays.

Peter 'The Cat' Bonetti was among the first to be targeted and his knee swelled up to twice its normal size after a robust challenge from Jones. The eventual outcome might have been different had the slightly-built Bonetti, now a coach with the England Under-21 squad, not possessed the indomitable courage which was the trademark of Sexton's side. Webb was to recall: 'When I saw the Cat's knee at half-time, I was afraid they would be sticking me in goal for the second half. I told the trainer Harry Medhurst, "Do a good job on him, mate, he looks better in the green jersey than I do."'

Bonetti carried on and when it went into extra-time after Jones had scored for Leeds and Osgood for Chelsea, Webb rose at the far post to meet a long throw from Hutchinson which scraped off Jack Charlton's head. 'It went in off my ear,' Webb said. 'My first reaction was to look round to see what the ref was doing. Leeds had a habit of appealing for every decision and I thought maybe they'd persuade him to rub it out. But the ref was pointing to the centre.'

EN ROUTE TO WEMBLEY 1970

THIRD ROUND
3 January
Chelsea 3   Birmingham 0

....

Chelsea: Bonetti, Webb, McCreadie, Hollins, Dempsey, Harris, Cooke, Hudson, Osgood (1), Hutchinson (2), Houseman.

Birmingham: Herriott, Martin, Thomson, Page, Robinson, Beard, Murray, Hockey, Hateley, Vowden, Vincent.

Attendance: 45,088

FOURTH ROUND
24 January
Chelsea 2   Burnley 2

....

Chelsea: Bonetti, Webb, McCreadie, Hollins (1), Dempsey, Harris, Baldwin, Hudson, Osgood (1), Hutchinson, Houseman.

Burnley: Mellor, Angus, Thomson, O'Neill, Dobson (2), Merrington, Casper, Coates, Wilson, Bellamy, Kindon.

Attendance: 48,282

FOURTH ROUND REPLAY
27 January
Burnley 1   Chelsea 3   (aet)

....

Burnley: Mellor, Angus, Thomson, O'Neill, Dobson, Merrington, Casper, Coates (1), Wilson, Bellamy, Kindon.

Chelsea: Bonetti, Webb, McCreadie, Hollins, Dempsey, Harris, Cooke, Hudson, Baldwin (1), Hutchinson, Houseman (2).

Attendance: 32,000

CUP TRIVIA

Apart from the trip to Turf Moor for the fourth round replay with Burnley, Chelsea played all their ties up until the Final replay in London. Burnley and Crystal Palace were the only First Division opponents they met prior to the Final.

Peter Osgood (pictured left) scored in every round of the competition, emulating Jeff Astle's (WBA) feat of two seasons earlier.

Chelsea's FA Cup success enabled them to compete in the following season's European Cup-Winners' Cup. They won that, too. In the final in Athens, they beat Real Madrid 2-1 after a replay with goals from John Dempsey and, inevitably, Osgood.

FIFTH ROUND
7 February
Crystal Palace 1   Chelsea 4

....

Crystal Palace: Jackson, Sewell, Loughlan, Payne, McCormick, Blyth, Hoadley, Taylor, Hynd, Queen, Hoy (1).

Chelsea: Bonetti, Webb, McCreadie, Hollins, Dempsey (1), Harris, Baldwin, Hudson, Osgood (1), Hutchinson (1), Houseman (1).

Attendance: 48,479

SIXTH ROUND
21 February
QPR 2   Chelsea 4

....

QPR: Kelly, Clement, Gillard, Watson, Mobley, Hazell, Bridges (1), Venables (1 pen), Leach, March, Ferguson.

Chelsea: Bonetti, Webb (1), McCreadie, Hollins, Dempsey, Harris, Baldwin, Hudson, Osgood (3), Hutchinson, Houseman.

Attendance: 33,572

SEMI-FINAL
14 March (at White Hart Lane)
Watford 1   Chelsea 5

....

Watford: Walker, Welbourne, Williams, Lugg, Lees, Walley, Scullion, Garbett (1), Endean, Packer, Owen (Garvey).

Chelsea: Bonetti, Webb (1), McCreadie, Hollins, Dempsey, Harris, Baldwin, Hudson, Osgood (1), Hutchinson (1), Houseman (2).

Attendance: 55,200

FA CUP FINAL
11 April (at Wembley)
Chelsea 2   Leeds 2   (aet)

....

Chelsea: Bonetti, Webb, McCreadie, Hollins, Dempsey, Harris (Hinton), Baldwin, Hudson, Osgood, Hutchinson (1), Houseman (1).

Leeds: Sprake, Madeley, Cooper, Bremner, Charlton (1), Hunter, Lorimer, Clarke, Jones (1), Giles, Gray.

Attendance: 100,000

FA CUP FINAL REPLAY
29 April (at Old Trafford)
Chelsea 2   Leeds 1   (aet)

....

Chelsea: Bonetti, Harris, McCreadie, Hollins, Dempsey, Webb (1), Baldwin, Cooke, Osgood (1) (Hinton), Hutchinson, Houseman.

Leeds: Harvey, Madeley, Cooper, Bremner, Charlton, Hunter, Lorimer, Clarke, Jones (1), Giles, Gray.

Attendance: 62,000

Strength of character, as much as ability, had enabled Sexton's side to keep coming back and eventually win against the most successful English side of the era, and Alan Hudson doubts now if Ruud Gullit's side can match them in that department. 'We saw it at places like Bolton and Leeds when they tended to lie down a bit,' he said. 'The time they did show character was against Wimbledon in the semi-final. They were ready for that one. But I thought Wimbledon weren't the Wimbledon of old. They'd played a lot of games in a short space of time and it affected them.'

Charlie Cooke, a highly intelligent man with a whimsical sense of humour, was the Zola figure in the 1970s side, and

Hudson says: 'I don't think you could really compare them. Charlie was a great player, a wonderful dribbler and excellent crosser. He didn't score as many goals as Zola, because he played wide. If he had played behind the front man like Zola does, he would have scored a lot more.'

The biggest difference between the sides, says Hudson, is that the 1997 side has no-one to compare with Peter Osgood. 'If Ossie was playing in the current side, they'd be contenders to win the title. He could score thirty or more goals a season. He was unbelievable. He had great service from Charlie and Peter Houseman, and I laid on a few for him. Mark Hughes is a

fine all-round player, but he doesn't get the goals Ossie got. I'd match him alongside Ian Hutchinson as a target man.

'In goal there's no comparison, Peter Bonetti was far better than any of today's goalkeepers at the Bridge. He was an exceptional talent. I played with Pat Jennings, Peter Shilton, Gordon Banks – and he's right up there with them.

'I'd have Webby, Ron Harris and Eddie McCreadie at the back any

How would the 1970 side have fared against the 1997 team? 'I think we would just have won!' said Hudson.

time, and I'd also find a place for Frank Leboeuf. He's the best in that role since Bobby Moore and I think he passes the ball more accurately than Moore over distance. Some of his sixty-yard passes are hit with the precision of a darts player.'

Hudson accepts that Dennis Wise and Roberto Di Matteo would be contenders for a place in midfield. 'Dennis Wise has had his best season and I'm surprised Glenn Hoddle didn't get him back in the England squad,' he said. 'He's matured a lot. He used to spend too much of his time getting involved with niggly things. Now he's suddenly become a very good footballer. He's controlled the bad side. Roberto Di Matteo is a very workman-like

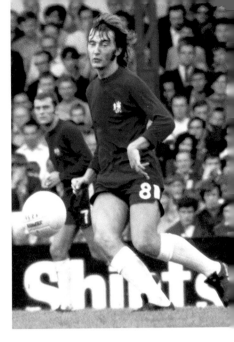

player, someone who can get forward and score goals. Charlie and I used to create a lot, and we would have created even more if Dave Sexton hadn't kept switching us about! John Hollins was there to supply the graft, and a good job he did of it.'

There is one player Hudson would make an automatic choice in his all-time best Chelsea XI - Ruud Gullit. 'He could get into any team in the world at his best, in any position. There's hardly been such a great all-round player. He could star anywhere. If he had kept fit, he could have stayed in the side and they would have been better for it.

'Being a player as well as a manager affected him, as it does them all. Bryan Robson had to pack up playing after six months as a manager. It's impossible these days to do both jobs properly. It's too tiring mentally.'

The other contender for a place in the Alan Hudson all-time XI would be Hoddle. 'Good enough to get in any side in any era,' he says. 'But if there is someone who didn't make it and should have done in my view, it was Colin Pates. He had the ability to play at the highest level but he was at the club at the wrong time with the wrong manager.'

How would the 1970 side have fared against the 1997 team? 'I think we would just have won!'

said Hudson. 'But it would have been a close thing. Where our team would have come out on top is in having more strong characters, particularly in defence.

'The present side hasn't got a David Webb, a Ron Harris or an Eddie McCreadie, the kind of players you need when you are playing against sides like Leeds on their own ground. If the 1997 side had played against the 1970 side in that FA Cup replay, I don't think they would have won.'

ABOVE: Alan Hudson was Chelsea's great unfulfilled talent, but some player!

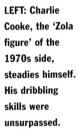

LEFT: Charlie Cooke, the 'Zola figure' of the 1970s side, steadies himself. His dribbling skills were unsurpassed.

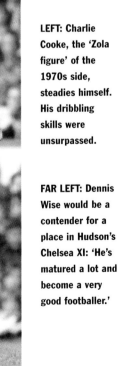

FAR LEFT: Dennis Wise would be a contender for a place in Hudson's Chelsea XI: 'He's matured a lot and become a very good footballer.'

Peter
Bonetti

Ron
Harris

John
Dempsey

Frank
Leboeuf

Eddie
McCreadie

Charlie
Cooke

Ray
Wilkins

Roberto
Di Matteo

Alan
Hudson

Jimmy
Greaves

Peter
Osgood

For his part, Peter Osgood ridicules suggestions that the side of the early seventies lacked dedication or fitness. 'No-one trained his players harder than Dave Sexton,' he said. 'He didn't have a lot of ability as a player himself, so he had to train harder to make up for it. One or two of the players might have celebrated a bit, but most of the stories were exaggerated. If we were as bad as that, we would never have been able to achieve what we did.'

'Dave was a brilliant coach who got us doing all the right things. Unfortunately he fell out with some of the players, otherwise we could have gone on and done even better. The main difference between then and now was that we played with two wingers in Charlie Cooke and Peter Houseman, whereas today it's wing-backs and they don't get so many crosses in. Football is all about crosses – the more you put in, the easier it is to score.

'If you chose eighteen players from both these squads you would have a great side. The one certainty to start would be Peter Bonetti. He was rightly classed as second best only to Gordon Banks, and Chelsea haven't had anyone as good as him before or since.

'Frank Leboeuf might make the starting line-up as well. He's not the greatest tackler but he hits some lovely balls out of defence, just like Bobby Moore.

'Zola would be a match-winner in any era. He looks tired sometimes, but that is because he makes so many runs. He is a player who gets everyone going and the goals he gets are spectacular.

LEFT: Peter Osgood fires in another effort on goal. 'If Ossie was playing in the current side, they'd be contenders to win the title,' says Alan Hudson.

CHELSEA MANAGERS

John Tait Robertson	**1905 – 1907**
David Calderhead	**1907 – 1933**
Leslie Knighton	**1933 – 1939**
Billy Birrell	**1939 – 1952**
Ted Drake	**1952 – 1961**
Tommy Docherty	**1961 – 1967**
Dave Sexton	**1967 – 1974**
Ron Suart	**1974 – 1975**
Eddie McCreadie	**1975 – 1977**
Ken Shellito	**1977 – 1978**
Danny Blanchflower	**1978 – 1979**
Geoff Hurst	**1979 – 1981**
John Neal	**1981 – 1985**
John Hollins	**1985 – 1988**
Bobby Campbell	**1988 – 1991**
Ian Porterfield	**1991 – 1993**
David Webb	**1993**
Glenn Hoddle	**1993 – 1996**
Ruud Gullit	**1996 –**

'Mark Hughes has blossomed in partnership with him,' Osgood points out. 'It's all about partnerships – Hutch and myself, Toshack and Keegan, whoever.'

After the triumphs in 1970 at Old Trafford and in Athens in the European Cup-Winners' Cup Final the following year, Chelsea were confidently expected to become a major force in English football. So why didn't it happen? 'The wrong decisions were made,' said Osgood. 'They spent a fortune on the East Stand and the team suffered. The place became a shambles.

'This time they're going about things in the right way. Ken Bates has had this dream and now he is on the way to seeing it realised.

There isn't a single player anywhere in the world who would turn down the chance to come to Chelsea now, and you couldn't say that four years ago. Ruud Gullit has got them playing some excellent football. He's won things in the game and nothing bothers him. He's so laid-back. He's helped the players to be more relaxed and confident and they can express themselves better. You can't do that when you're wound up and nervous.

'He's made his money and he's not in management to make more. He's in it for the glory and that's got to be a good thing for Chelsea. He's not satisfied . . . he wants more.'

CHELSEA'S UPS AND DOWNS

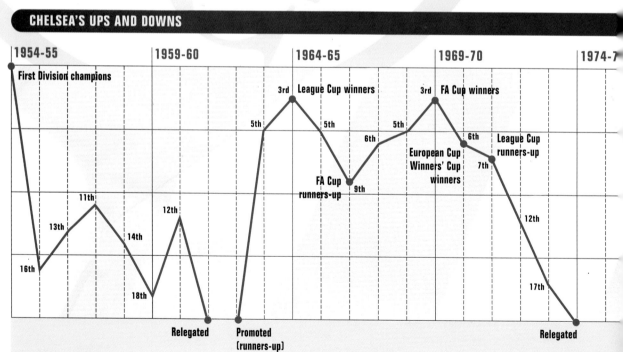

| 1954-55 | 1959-60 | 1964-65 | 1969-70 | 1974-7 |

First Division champions

3rd — League Cup winners

3rd — FA Cup winners

5th

5th

5th

6th

6th — League Cup runners-up

European Cup Winners' Cup winners

7th

FA Cup runners-up — 9th

11th

13th

12th

14th

12th

16th

18th

17th

Relegated

Promoted (runners-up)

Relegated

LEFT: Ruud Gullit is mobbed by Chelsea fans as he comes down the steps at Wembley, having led the club to its first major trophy for 26 years. But as Peter Osgood says, 'He's not satisfied. He wants more.'

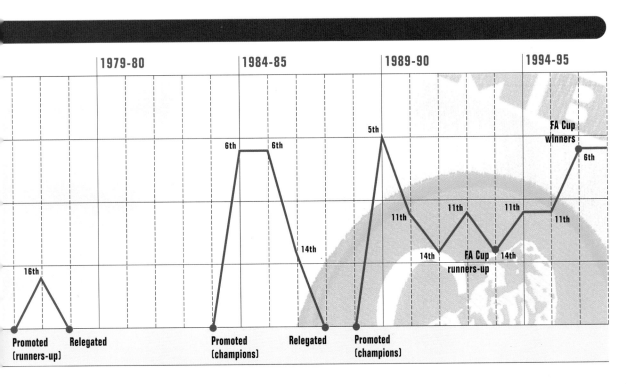

| 1979-80 | 1984-85 | 1989-90 | 1994-95 |

FA Cup winners

5th

6th 6th

11th 11th 11th 11th 6th

14th 14th 14th

FA Cup runners-up

16th

Promoted (runners-up)   Relegated   Promoted (champions)   Relegated   Promoted (champions)

MATTHEW HARDING R.I.P.

Just after midnight on Wednesday, October 23, my telephone rang and someone on the *Daily Mail* newsdesk said a helicopter had crashed in Cheshire and it was believed that Matthew Harding was on board. Was there any way of checking that this was so? I could only confirm that Matthew Harding often flew by helicopter to Chelsea's away matches but there was no way of establishing whether he was a passenger. The police had similar problems.

The chartered Eurocopter Twin Squirrel had come down in an open field 400 yards from Norcroft Farm near Middlewich just off the M6. It should have been heading south towards London but was flying in a north-easterly direction, possibly indicating that the pilot was aware of a problem and was aiming to make an emergency landing. The 999 calls to police had not been able to identify a precise location for

the crash and they had to use a light aircraft to find out where it had come down. The almost unrecognisable bodies of five men were discovered close together but the helicopter had disintegrated, scattering debris over a 400-yard radius. The fuselage had ploughed on for nearly 100 yards before bursting into flames.

The first clue emerged when one of the searchers found a charred piece of paper with the word 'Burnden' on it - Burnden Park, the old Bolton Wanderers ground. Chelsea had lost there 2-1 in a League

Cup tie and Matthew Harding had been present with three friends: Raymond Deane, 43, from Camberley, Surrey; John Bauldie, 47, of Richmond, Surrey; and Tony Burridge, 39, of Wimbledon, south London. The pilot, who also died, was Michael Goss, 38, of Wilton, Salisbury.

On the flight up to Bolton, they had stopped off near the factory of the hot-air balloonist Per Lindstrand in Oswestry, Shropshire. Lindstrand was working on the balloon which Richard Branson was planning to take on a trip later in the winter, and Harding was one of the sponsors of the project. The Virgin hot-air balloon was destined to come down, safely, in North Africa. Lindstrand said: 'It was not a night to be flying in a helicopter. I would not have flown to Bolton and back in those conditions.'

At 4.30pm the helicopter took off, bound for Bolton. It landed in the car park of Warburton's bakery on the outskirts of the town and Jonathon Warburton, one of the directors, took the party to a pub. Harding always liked a drink before matches. 'Matthew was cracking jokes all through the game,' said Warburton. 'When Chelsea scored, he was jumping up and down and I told him to sit down.'

Though Chelsea lost, Harding was in good spirits when the

RIGHT: Matthew Harding as he would like to be remembered, celebrating another Chelsea victory.

FAR LEFT: Outside the entrance to Stamford Bridge, the floral tributes to Harding pile up, both from Chelsea fans and supporters of other clubs.

helicopter took off just after 11pm. Police said the weather conditions at the time were good.

Next morning, when it was established that Harding, the country's 89th richest man according to the *Sunday Times*, had perished in the crash, there was a feeling of shock throughout the land. Tributes poured in from all quarters, from Prime Minister John Major, who said Harding would be terribly missed, and Prime Minister-in-waiting Tony Blair, whose New Labour Party

had just benefited to the extent of £1 million from Harding's generosity.

'This is an appalling tragedy,' said Blair. 'He was so full of life and vigour and someone deeply committed to his country.'

A supporter, Nicky Nakrja, said: 'To us Chelsea fans he was like a godfather. He gave us hope and spirit in the team, which he built up with his money.'

Richard Branson said: 'Matthew was full of life and it is tragic that he lost it so young.'

LEFT: One of the quieter times in the tempestuous relationship of Harding and Ken Bates (left).

BELOW: Harding pictured with manager Glenn Hoddle (left). He believed that Hoddle must be given money to improve the team.

BOTTOM RIGHT: Bates opens the new Chelsea Megastore in July 1997. He was determined to maximise the club's revenue.

Yet just over three years earlier, few people outside the square mile of the City of London had heard of Matthew Harding. He was born in Haywards Heath, Sussex, on December 26, 1953, the son of a Lloyd's underwriter, Paul Harding, who was a lifelong Chelsea supporter. Matthew's father took him to Stamford Bridge for the first time at the age of eight, and he became a fanatical supporter.

Going to Stamford Bridge provided the only hours of pleasure for a boy who was desperately miserable at his boarding school, Abingdon. 'He was quite unhappy here,' said his headmaster Michael St John Parker. 'He thought of himself as being rejected and condemned as a failure by the school. A lot of that was in his own mind but he felt it pretty strongly.'

His academic record was a modest one - just one A level, in Latin. 'He was more noticed for reading the financial pages and he was keen on football,' said a teacher. When he left Abingdon, he went to work in a bank in Haywards Heath where, as he later said, his most onerous task was to shut the main doors at the end of the working day. A few tedious months later, he went to work in the Anglo-Portuguese Bank in Bishopsgate. After overstaying his lunchtime break in a pub, he was told to leave.

His life changed in 1973 when his father introduced him to Ted Benfield, who was setting up a reinsurance broking company. 'I think he had been sacked from several jobs and I gave him a job as a favour to his father,' said Benfield, 'who asked me to try and sort him out. Matthew arrived for the interview with shoulder-length hair and I told him to get it cut. He could come over as very pleasant and very talkative - let's say I taught him everything I knew, and he responded. He was a sort of rebel. I think the younger generation liked him. He tended to divide those who came across him, some loved him and some hated him. There was no halfway house with Matthew.'

Seven years afterwards, at the age of 27, Harding was given the opportunity to buy 10 per cent of the company's shares and two years later he bought out Benfield after borrowing £160,000 to buy a 32 per cent stake. By taking risks, Harding expanded the company at an incredible rate and by the early 1990s it was worth £150 million.

His life changed again in 1994 when he met Chelsea chairman Ken Bates and agreed to loan the club much-needed cash to buy players and build the stand which is now named after him. Harding was on the roller-coaster ride upwards taken by Robert Maxwell, Alan Sugar and others before him:

successful businessmen who become national figures through involvement with a football club. Mohammed Al Fayed is the latest to step on. A keen self-publicist, Harding now found himself being courted by most of the younger football reporters on the national newspapers, eager to know his plans for making Chelsea another Manchester United.

He was built up as 'one of us' by journalists and fans alike. Before matches, he drank at the Imperial Arms in the King's Road and chatted with supporters. He became their hero very quickly and Bates, the man who had kept the club alive, was cast as the villain. The fans thought Harding was putting millions of his personal fortune into the club: £26 million, it was said. It was a scenario that matched the expansive mood of football at the time, that rich men were still there to come along and bail ailing football clubs out with their largesse, all out of the goodness of their heart – because they loved the club. To have 'ambition', football clubs needed to have these entrepreneurs to fund them.

Bates knew differently. But whereas Harding monopolised the sports pages, Bates's publicity was in the main adverse. He did not have Harding's flair for it and frequently upset the writers with his sharp, barbed comments and

jibes in his programme notes. It rapidly developed into a PR battle between the two and Harding took an early lead which he never relinquished. He made it clear to those close to him that he wanted to take control of the club. The snag was that Bates still possessed the majority of the shares and had no intention of giving up. By this time Harding was a member of the Board, conducting a power struggle from within and without.

Bates had a vision of turning the twelve acres of Stamford Bridge, less than fifteen minutes' drive from the centre of London, into a complex that would generate enough income to support a football club ready to challenge the Manchester Uniteds and Liverpools.

As he told Jimmy Greaves in an interview in *The Sun* in March 1997: 'We were fifteen years behind United because we wasted so much time fighting property developers, then dealing with Matthew Harding. He held us up with that power struggle. He put one and one together and came up with one and a half. He could have had it all, had he waited, but he was badly advised into taking me on.

'We paid interest on his loans and made him £40 million from his shares. When I asked him to give me a business plan for everything he said he was going to do, he did a runner. Last June we gave him all his money back and said, "Let's work together." And to be fair, we were until he died. But we've spent £8 million on players since we gave him his money back.'

When he was conducting journalists around the 'new' Bridge before the Cup Final, the chairman said: 'This is a business I know. I designed this ground and the architects just did the

RIGHT: Managing director Colin Hutchinson poses proudly in front of the new South Stand at the old Shed End.

OVERLEAF: The East Stand lies empty and a wreath occupies Matthew Harding's usual seat on the day of the match against Spurs, Chelsea's first after his death.

drawings. I was in construction, and my time at Wigan and Oldham stood me in good stead when I came here. Maybe every chairman should have to do it. I was ready for the battle, and that's just as well because nothing has gone smoothly since we got here. It took us ten years to get off the ground, four years to get planning permission. We had no continuity, everything was hand-to-mouth. We were a small club with a clapped-out ground. Our rivals were Crystal Palace and QPR, not Arsenal or Spurs.'

Irving Scholar had tried to diversify into other areas when he was chairman of Tottenham Hotspur, and many of his plans went awry. But the City analysts had no similar fears as more ideas

poured out of Stamford Bridge. Chelsea Village bought its own travel company EDT for £2.3 million to transport its fans abroad. It also launched its own credit card. More than 60,000 people parted with £25 to become club members. Nearly half of the 56 apartments in the complex went in the first few weeks, with the prime one being reserved for

Bates himself. The hotel was rapidly taking shape. Underground there was a car park to bring in more cash.

The feud between Harding and Bates had reached its climax when the chairman banned his rival from the directors' box. Harding won the sympathy vote in the press the next morning and was accompanied by a squad of news

reporters when he tried to turn up to take his seat in the stand. He had also been banned from the dressing-room, but football reporters waiting to interview players in the corridor leading from there spotted him going through a fire exit to beat the ban. An hour later he emerged looking triumphant. 'I've had a nice chat with Glenn Hoddle,' he said.

Harding was a hyperactive, enthusiastic type of person, hard to dislike. He talked so much and showed such passion that one wondered what he was really like. After his death, the mystery remained. His private life was a tangled one, with a wife and devoted family in Ditchling, Sussex, and a mistress and child in London.

The day it was confirmed he had died, thousands of supporters of all ages turned up at Stamford Bridge, many laying wreaths and flowers against the gates. The grief was genuine, almost like it was when John F Kennedy died at a similar age.

Harding's three years at Chelsea had been an extraordinary episode. His memorial service at the Queen Elizabeth II Conference Centre in Westminster was staged in a manner which would have appealed to him. The 300 invited guests were greeted by Harding's face on a large screen. 'Forever Young' by his favourite singer Bob Dylan was played as the lights dimmed. Each seat had a Chelsea matchday programme on it and a video showed him celebrating a Chelsea goal.

His friend Tom Watt, the actor and journalist, said: 'None of the fans will ever forget Matthew, who dreamed along with them for 25 years and then did everything he could to make their dreams come true. Matthew was a fan first and last, the rest was simply done because he was able to do it.'

The service was conducted by the Rev. Steve Chalke, international director of the homeless charity Oasis Trust with which Harding was involved. 'The last thing he would have wanted was a morbid service,' the Rev. Chalke said. As they left, mourners were handed a glass of Harding's favourite ale with a picture of him on it, toasting Chelsea.

Bates was in Egypt on holiday at the time. 'I suppose I've got an image of being big, bad Ken Bates,' he said. 'It would be nice to have a big, good image instead. Part of the problem was the press campaign orchestrated by Harding, and all sorts of people joined in. Well, none of these developments are down to him. The loans he gave us have all been repaid. On June 26 last year, I met him in the Dorchester Hotel and gave him a bank draft for £2.7 million, which was what we owed him.'

The much-revered Harding, loved by many and despised by a few, had gone, but other more anonymous investors were moving in to help finance the building of the new complex and new ground. After years of stagnation, Chelsea Football Club was at last moving into the 21st century at an incredible pace.

For Ruud Gullit, for Ken Bates, for everyone connected with the club, the future is bright.

The future is Chelsea.

ABOVE LEFT: An emotional day for Matthew's widow Ruth Harding, hands clasped to her face, in the directors' box at the Spurs match.

RIGHT: This fan does not forget Matthew Harding on FA Cup Final day at Wembley. The crowd still sing of 'his' blue and white army.

Acknowledgments

Sincere thanks are due to Gwyn Williams, Chelsea's Chief Administrative Officer, for his valuable assistance, and also Peter Osgood, Alan Hudson, Ron Greenwood, and others too numerous to mention.

Thanks also to Chelsea's Managing Director, Colin Hutchinson and his staff.

Last but not least, at publishers HarperCollins I am eternally grateful to editor Tom Whiting, designer Paul Calver and project editor Charles Richards for their hard work and support throughout the writing of this book.